HOW TO BECOME A MYSTERY SHOPPER

THE ONLY BOOK YOU'LL EVER NEED

Elaine Moran

How to Become a Mystery Shopper, The Only Book You'll Ever Need
Copyright © 2008 by Mystery Shoppers Training Group

ISBN 978-0-9777365-1-5
EAN 9780977736515
Library of Congress 2005939164

Cover Photography by Katya Williams www.KatyaWilliams.com

2nd Edition 2008
Published by Mystery Shoppers Training Group
California, USA www.MysteryShoppersTraining.com

ABOUT THE AUTHOR

I have been a Mystery Shopper for over twenty five years. I am actively involved in Mystery Shopping and I also present workshops and lectures throughout the world on How to Become a Mystery Shopper. This book contains information taken from my background in business, education, training, and as a hands-on Mystery Shopper. My experience as a college instructor, entrepreneur, and world traveler will help to make the information contained in this book come alive for you, the reader.

In 1982 while browsing through a popular women's magazine, I came across an article about a company engaged in Mystery Shopping. I was intrigued. I called the company, spoke with the owner, and by the following week I had received my first Mystery Shopping assignment.

I was sent to a trendy, high end department store in Beverly Hills, California and bought some very expensive place mats. I came home, put the stylish and "free" mats on my table, collected a shopping fee, and fell in love with the idea of getting paid and being a "spy." From that point on, I have actively pursued assignments as a Mystery Shopper while continuing my profession as a business owner and as an instructor of business courses.

In 1996 I was considering early retirement. I decided to offer a class on Mystery Shopping at the college with which I was affiliated. The proposal met with an enthusiastic response and since that time, I have been offering these classes and full day workshops to colleges in three western states and give talks on the subject of Mystery Shopping in many other localities throughout of the world.

My husband and I travel frequently and we present these workshops and lectures as a team. If you are unable to personally attend one of my workshops, this book will get you well on your way toward success in this exciting, important, and interesting career. For more information about the locations for upcoming classes, please visit our website at www.MysteryShoppersTraining.com.

It is always heartwarming for me to hear from participants after the workshops. Here are just a few of their comments.

- ❖ *"Really informative. Five Star."* B.P., Teacher
- ❖ *"This will be a life-changing experience for me."* H.R., Retired
- ❖ *"A wealth of information."* L.C., Attorney
- ❖ *"Dispelled all myths about Mystery Shoppers."* J.T., Nurse
- ❖ *"Elaine is an enthusiastic advocate for shopping."* S.C., Housewife

Thank you to my family for their support, encouragement and editing skills. And special mention to Herb, my husband and partner, without whom life would, indeed, be a lot less rewarding.

CONTENTS

3   Writing Reports

4 Understanding Guidelines

5 Sample Evaluations and Assignments

6 Becoming an Independent Contractor

7 Additional Helpful Information

8 Directories

9 Wrap Up

DEDICATION

This book is dedicated to everyone who wants to be part of this growing industry and help to improve customer service and business productivity. Whatever your age, education, or background, you will find the contents of this book to be interesting and, I hope, a stepping stone towards a new and exciting journey.

Mystery Shopping has been around for hundreds of years and now with the advent of instant web based communication via the personal computer, businesses throughout the world have the added advantage of almost immediate feedback in helping customers experience a more positive and enjoyable shopping experience.

I am writing this book to help you better understand some of the dynamics involved in Mystery Shopping.

I have been featured in newspapers across the country and have had the good fortune of sharing my experiences with thousands of interested participants from all walks of life. At the beginning of my workshops, I always ask the attendees why they are interested in becoming a Mystery Shopper. Here are some of their most frequent responses.

- ❖ Help Improve Customer Service
- ❖ Flexible Hours
- ❖ Fun
- ❖ Exciting
- ❖ Become Part of the Process
- ❖ Earn Extra Money
- ❖ Experience New Situations
- ❖ Get Free Stuff
- ❖ Open New Doors

If these sound like responses you can relate to, and you want to become involved in this exciting field, read on. Learn about the dynamics of Mystery Shopping and try some of the practice exercises. Let's get started on the road to Becoming a Mystery Shopper!

Elaine Moran
Mystery Shoppers Training Group
www.MysteryShoppersTraining.com

CONSUMER ALERT

You do not have to pay money to anyone to get into the Mystery Shopping business. Legitimate Mystery Shopping assignments are available for free.

You may be tempted by unsolicited emails or newspaper ads or radio commercials that claim you can earn a living as a secret shopper, earn $50 per hour or $100,000 per year. Beware! The Federal Trade Commission (FTC), the nation's consumer protection agency, tells us those marketers who promise lucrative jobs as Mystery Shoppers often do not deliver bona fide opportunities. These solicitations often promote websites where consumers can "register" to become Mystery Shoppers—AFTER paying a fee for information.

Consumers who seek to get a refund from such promoters of Mystery Shopping jobs are usually out of luck. Either the business does not return phone calls, or if it does, it is to try another pitch. It is rare that your money will produce many legitimate or worthwhile contacts.

BE SKEPTICAL OF MYSTERY SHOPPING PROMOTERS WHO:

- Advertise for Mystery Shoppers in free local throw-away advertising newspapers.
- Solicit for shoppers through non-referral emails
- Guarantee a job as a Mystery Shopper.
- Charge a fee to become a Mystery Shopper.
- Sell directories of Mystery Shopping companies.
- Offer to send your name to hundreds of Mystery Shopping companies.

> BECOMING A MYSTERY SHOPPER FOR A LEGITIMATE MYSTERY SHOPPING COMPANY SHOULD NOT COST YOU ANYTHING!

See Chapter 7 Too good to be True for additional information on Scams

1

WHAT IS A MYSTERY SHOPPER?

Mystery Shoppers visit businesses as ordinary customers.

Mystery Shoppers provide detailed evaluations of their experiences based on the guidelines provided by the Mystery Shopping company.

WHY DO COMPANIES NEED MYSTERY SHOPPERS?

Other terms such as secret shopper, performance evaluator, and auditor are occasionally used, but there is often no difference between those terms and/or "Mystery Shopper."

The purpose of a business is to provide a competitive service or product and make a profit for its owners. Businesses want to attract and retain customers. How does one company gain the edge over their competitors? How does a business keep customers coming back again and again?

One of the ways companies learn about their business as perceived from a customer's point of view is to hire "Mystery Shoppers." This can give them an insight into how the average customer views and experiences their business. Mystery Shoppers are not always hired because of their expertise in any particular industry, but frequently because they fit the profile of the average customer that the business is trying to attract. In addition, they are often able to bring a fresh, outside perspective on the company's operation.

Mystery Shopper or Private Investigator?

Keep in mind that as a Mystery Shopper you are NOT a Private Investigator. The companies hire Mystery Shoppers to perform a service to help them improve their business. A Private Investigator (PI) is hired to investigate wrongdoings, usually on behalf of an attorney or insurance company. Most states and local jurisdictions require PI's to be licensed.

A few states may also require Mystery Shoppers to be Private Investigators. You will need to check with the licensing department in your State to be sure you can work as a Mystery Shopper without being a PI. The Mystery Shopping company that plans to hire you may be able to provide you with that information.

Companies want to know how to improve the service they offer.

What procedures and products are they getting wrong or right? Are customers being greeted when they arrive in the store? Are they offered assistance? Can the employee answer questions regarding the products being displayed and sold? Is the store clean? Did the shopper find it

14

comfortable and easy to shop? Would the customer want to return? Why?

Companies want to know what the competition is doing.

Does a similar store down the street offer a better service, an additional incentive? What is being offered? How long did it take to receive service there compared to the service we offer?

Companies want to know if there are specific problems that need to be addressed.

What is the problem? Are the lights bright enough? Are the aisles too tight? Is the merchandise dirty? Is the music too loud? Are there boxes blocking the shelves?

Companies want to know if there are any employees that merit special recognition.

Did the employees offer excellent service? Did they smile? Did they make eye contact? Was there any particular employee that stood out and helped to enhance the shopper's experience?

Outstanding employees are often rewarded. As a Mystery Shopper, you are part of the process to help the best employees become recognized by management as well as help them identify needed improvements. If an employee does not provide excellent service, then the feedback you provide can be used as a training tool for that employee. In the long run, everyone benefits from the reports generated by Mystery Shoppers.

As a Mystery Shopper you are providing a professional service by submitting an unbiased and informative report on your observations. Enjoy the experience.

––––––––––

"A great many customers will not return bad service with bad behavior...They just never come back."
> Connelly, James H.R. *Close to the Customer*. Homewood, Illinois: Business One Irwin

WHAT TYPES OF BUSINESSES USE MYSTERY SHOPPERS

If an employee works with the public, chances are they will be "mystery shopped." The list of businesses that utilize Mystery Shopping services is almost endless. Among the many businesses frequently using Mystery Shoppers you will find:

Hotels
Convenience Stores
Movie Theatres
Health Clubs
Banks
Restaurants
Florists
Home Developers
Car Dealerships
Auto Repair Shops
Rental Car Companies
Golf Courses
Department Stores
Rental Developments
Gas Stations
Pet Stores
Resorts
Spas
Services
Medical/Health Care
Government Agencies
New Home Builders

As you can see, the possibilities are unlimited and the list continues to grow as more industries adopt this practice.

"Service is the hottest subject in business right now, but most of the service is lip service, not customer service."
> Glen, Peter It's *Not My Department! How to Get the Service You Want, Exactly the Way You Want It.* New York: William Murray and Company, Inc

HOW DOES IT WORK?

Let's take a look at the Mystery Shopping process.

Retail or service companies enter into contracts with Mystery Shopping firms to help them evaluate their business practices. Years ago, most businesses had their own in-house department to monitor their various stores. Now, with so many mega corporations and franchisors, and to foster objectively defensible evaluations, many businesses have discontinued using their own staff as Mystery Shoppers. They rely on Mystery Shopping companies to fill their needs wherever they are located. There are thousands of Mystery Shopping companies located throughout the world.

The Mystery Shopping companies do not need to be located in your specific area of the country in order to offer shopping opportunities in your particular home town. For instance, you might live in Dubuque, Iowa and work for a company that is located in Seattle, Washington. I work for several companies that offer shopping opportunities in my area of Southern California, and yet these Mystery Shopping companies are based in Australia and Canada.

The Mystery Shopping companies have networks of shoppers in every geographical area that they service. For example, if they have a client that has 50 stores in St. Louis that need to be mystery shopped, the Mystery Shopping company refers to its database of available Mystery Shoppers in the St. Louis area and offers them the opportunity to accept or decline the specific assignments. In order to be in the database for that Mystery Shopping company, you will need to fill out an application—and we will cover that process later on in this manual.

A typical Mystery Shopping assignment might have you going into a retail business, restaurant, rental apartment complex, grocery store, bank or hotel and interacting with the employees. You will then report on the interaction noting the level of customer service you received, the timeliness of your transaction, the cleanliness of the products, and more. In addition to the "typical" shops, there are many other types which you will read about later in this book.

Imagine, you can do Mystery Shops while at home in your town, wherever it is! And then, while you're vacationing in Paris, London, Denver, or Timbuktu, you can take assignments there and that can not only be fun, but can help defer some of your vacation costs.

Mystery Shopping companies retain a staff of booking agents or SCHEDULERS who will contact you regarding available assignments in your area. The scheduler will be your personal link to the Mystery Shopping company. Most schedulers are themselves, independent contractors and often face a difficult challenge in fulfilling all the assignments for their many locations. You should always try to cooperate and make their job easier.

There will be one other very important person in the Mystery Shopping company with whom you will be working. That is the EDITOR. When you turn in a report, the editor will review it and make sure it meets the retail client's expectations and is up to the retailer's standards. Hopefully you never get to know the editor very well because they will usually only contact you if there is a problem with your report or if they have a question that you did not adequately cover in your report.

Shoppers are often graded and rated on their reports, so it is important that you read and understand the directions you are given prior to performing a shop. Every company has its own method of grading and rating a shopper. The most common one is on a scale from one to ten. Usually, if you can keep your score at seven or above, you will become a preferred shopper. As we go through this book, we will cover several examples of assignments and show you sample reports. It will be beneficial for you to start off on this new career with as much knowledge as possible. My goal is for everyone reading this book to become a "perfect 10."

"The delivery of quality service is never the customer's job."
    Connelly, James H.R. *Close to the Customer* Homewood, Illinois, Business One Irwin

HOW IS THE PAY?

Please don't expect to get rich as a Mystery Shopper. It will not happen! Be careful of ads you see promising fifty dollars an hour and up as a Mystery Shopper. Be careful of ads wanting to charge you for lists and information. They may be misleading. Keep in mind that a Mystery Shopping company NEVER charges you to work for them. If you want to believe that you can make a lot of money as a Mystery Shopper, you will be disappointed. Although there are occasions when you can make at least $50 per hour and/or several hundred dollars for less than a day's work, those situations are not frequent and usually are available to more experienced shoppers.

Here's a reality check for you.

The average pay for a retail shop is $10 to $20 per report.
You may or may not be reimbursed an additional small amount for a product.

The average pay for a bank shop is $20 to $40 per report and it may require a lengthy report.

The average pay for a grocery store is $9 to $25 per report.
You may or may not received reimbursement for some groceries.

The average restaurant shop reimburses you for meals for two.
You may or may not be paid an additional fee.

The average hotel shop will reimburse you for a one or two night stay.
You may or may not be paid an additional fee.

The average golf shop will reimburse you for a round of golf.
You may or may not be paid an additional fee.

The time it takes to actually do a shop ranges from ten minutes to an hour. Sometimes more!

The time it takes to complete an evaluation form ranges from ten minutes to three or four hours, depending on the type of assignment you accept.

But keep in mind that you get to choose which types of assignments you prefer. If you write well and type quickly, and if you like to write a lot of narrative, then you can choose the long, detailed reports. If you only prefer to complete a simple checkbox or fill-in-the-blanks type of form, then you can choose and stick with only those assignments.

You will need to pay for the products, meals, hotels, etc., and any other types of shops which you choose, out of your own pocket and get reimbursed after you submit your receipts and reports. It often takes a month or more to receive your reimbursement. Of course some companies pay sooner but some take as long as ninety days. You will learn of their payment policy prior to accepting an assignment.

Don't be discouraged by the seemingly low pay. There are many ways to schedule the shops to your advantage and make it more profitable. For instance, when I take a shop at a certain mall, I continue to watch other Mystery Shopping company websites and emails for more shops in that same area or mall so that when I do actually go out on my shopping trip, I will have three or four shops to do at one time. I also usually try to add a lunch shop in the mix so I end up having a fun day at the mall, a nice lunch out, and some extra money on top of the free products or services.

My husband tells me that the difference between most people and me is that when they go to the mall they pay, and when I go to the mall I get paid! I hope that after reading this book, you'll be right alongside me, enjoying yourself at the mall as a Mystery Shopper and getting paid, too!

It is better not to enter the Mystery Shopping field expecting to make more money than the average executive or professional with an advanced professional degree. Try to maintain the attitude that this is extra, "found" money that comes from experiencing a new and exciting adventure. It may not be steady, it may not be lucrative, but it will keep you active, involved, and smiling.

And there are bonuses! Bonuses are sometimes offered for shops located in out-of-the-way areas or when deadlines approach and the schedulers are eager to get the shop assigned within a specific timeline. This is a nice way to add extra income. But, you won't get those bonuses unless you have proven yourself to be dependable.

TYPES OF ASSIGNMENTS

You will have opportunities to shop at stores you've never been to before, eat at restaurants that you've always wanted to try, or stay overnight at a special hotel or resort. Or perhaps you can shop several of the grocery stores in your area and take advantage of their sales while making some extra money. The choices and experiences are unlimited. And, you get to choose when and where!

After twenty five years of Mystery Shopping, you might assume that I would be bored and feeling stuck in a rut doing the same thing over and over again. Wrong! Actually, each week presents a new opportunity, a new type of shop, a place I've never been to before, or a type of assignment I've never done.

Lest you think only of the standard shop as one where you purchase an item and then write an evaluation afterward, take note that there is so much more! This past year I have seen shopping assignments where one gets to take their family of eight to the circus, or visit the Auto Show and see all the new cars, or go to a furniture wholesaler and pretend to be a decorator, or pretend you're out-of-work and apply for a job to see if a company complies with all the various employment regulations. These are just a few I selected from a large number of recent Mystery Shopping opportunities.

I would like to share some of these recent assignments that have been available on various Mystery Shopping job postings. Some are Mystery Shopping; some cover other aspects of information gathering. I've accepted some of these assignments and others I declined. You will see that there are always options for you to select the types of assignments that are best suited to you and your needs.

The Directory at the end of this book will give you the website addresses to enable you find similar postings plus many more. A complete list of types and amounts of assignments offered would be too lengthy for me to list here.

Reimbursements and fees may vary by location.

THEATRES. Visit the lobby of your local theater. Note if they offer popcorn in specific bags. Pays $10

SENIOR HOUSING. Telephone and visit to inquire for yourself or parent. Pays $95.

FAMILY PORTRAIT. Have pictures taken and buy a package. $100 reimbursement.

TAKE-OUT RESTAURANT. Purchase several drinks and return the empty cups to the Mystery Shopping company. Pays $5 plus reimbursement for drinks.

RESTAURANT PHONE CALLS. Call approximately 15 restaurants to get the price of standard breakfast, lunch and dinner. Pays $50.

RECALL. Pick up damaged product from consumer, purchase additional items at the same retailer, return to manufacturer. Pays $12 to $15 per hour plus mileage and reimbursement.

FLEET VEHICLES. Note condition of vehicles, employee uniforms, and sign placements. Need tape measure and camera. Pays $55.

VALET PARKING. Park your car for minimum of half an hour. Pays $15 to $20 plus reimbursement.

FAST FOOD RESTAURANT. Purchase a meal. If the employee offers to upsize your meal, you award them a cash bonus on the spot. Reimbursement plus pays $10

MEDICAL EXAM. Take a medical exam at a licensed employment medical office. Reimbursement for exam plus small fee for report.

HORSEBACK RIDING. Spend an hour horseback riding. Reimbursement for two plus $15.

LUXURY CAR DEALERS. Visit four competing car dealers in one day and inquire about a car. Pays $120.

PLAY BINGO. Take the tour bus to a casino, order food and drinks, play bingo. Reimbursement plus $35 and keep your winnings!

EXIT INTERVIEWS. Four separate locations. Interview customers as they leave store. $125 day.

TRANSPORTATION. Pack your bag and purchase a ticket. Do not use. Evaluate customer service. Reimbursement plus $25.

WEDDING GOWN. Shop for a wedding gown. Pays $28 plus bonus if completed by deadline.

CHAIN RESTAURANTS. Offers up to $75 bonuses for out of the way locations.

CAR INSURANCE. Pretend you have a poor driving record and shop for car insurance. Pays $20.

TOILETS. Take pictures of inside of toilets at various restaurants to capture the flushing and sanitizing action. Must have digital camera.

TABLES AND CHAIRS. Visit restaurants and count tables and chairs. $15 per restaurant.

HAIR LOSS. Visit clinic. Must not have a full head of hair! Pays $25

TRUCK STOP. Purchase gas at a truck stop, buy something in the convenience store, have lunch or dinner in the dining room, take a shower or (pretend to take a shower). Evaluate all of the sections. Reimbursement plus $15 fee.

GROCERY STORE. Purchase several grocery items. Place one of the items on the bottom of the basket. If the employee does not notice it, call it to their attention. $15 reimbursement plus $5 fee.

WHAT DOES IT TAKE TO BECOME A MYSTERY SHOPPER?

As a Mystery Shopper, the most important thing to remember is that YOU MUST FOLLOW DIRECTIONS. You will be given an assignment and guidelines to follow by the scheduler or the Mystery Shopping company. You must carefully read the guidelines, be sure you understand them, and then do exactly as you are instructed. As a Mystery Shopper, it is not your role to tell a company how they should run their business.

Approach the assignment in a positive way. You are looking for the hidden gems; the employees who do their job well. The company may have a policy that the employees must greet each customer within a minute after they enter the store. You will check to see if that is actually happening. Or the company may have a policy that says there should be no handwritten signs on doors or windows. You will check to make sure that all the signage is professionally printed. Your job is made easier since you do not have to make the rules.

Here are questions that require positive answers from an aspiring Mystery Shopper:

- ❖ Are you conscientious?

- ❖ Are you reliable?

- ❖ Can you meet deadlines?

- ❖ Can you write an objective report?

- ❖ Are you observant?

- ❖ Can you fit into new or challenging situations?

- ❖ Can you read and understand directions?

In addition you should have a good writing skills and the ability to use the computer and the internet.

> If you answered yes to all of these questions, then you meet some of the most important requirements to become a Mystery Shopper

MYSTERY SHOPPING
SECRETS REVEALED

To give you some insight into the minds of those who own Mystery Shopping companies, here are a few responses by several owners who were interviewed.

QUESTION: WHAT WILL MAKE US BETTER SHOPPERS

You must be able to read and understand the directions. Each client has different requirements and you must adhere to their specific guidelines.

QUESTION: WHAT CAN YOU SAY TO MYSTERY SHOPPERS IN GENERAL?

Be reliable and take a long-term approach to your work. Good shoppers get more work.

QUESTION: HOW MANY MYSTERY SHOPPING COMPANIES ARE THERE?

There are thousands of companies located in every part of the world.

QUESTION: HOW MANY SHOPPERS DO YOU HAVE IN YOUR DATABASE?

We have 9,000 shoppers in our database. Some larger companies have close to 150,000 shoppers. We perform 6,000 shops each month.

QUESTION: HOW MANY SHOPPERS ARE THERE IN THE UNITED STATES?

There are probably close to one million shoppers signed up with many different Mystery Shopping companies. A small percentage of these shoppers are considered excellent shoppers. So, as you can see, there is always room for new shoppers.

QUESTION: DO WE HAVE TO PAY TO SIGN UP WITH YOUR COMPANY?

No. Legitimate companies should not charge you to sign up with them.

QUESTION: WHY ARE THE APPLICATION FORMS SO LONG?

If someone is not willing to take the time to fill out our application, they certainly won't be able to complete our reports.

QUESTION: HOW DO YOU KNOW WHO THE GOOD SHOPPERS ARE?

We have a rating system and you are rated as a shopper. Shoppers with higher ratings will get more work.   Shoppers who do not fulfill their assignments will receive low scores and not be contacted again.

QUESTION: DO THE SCHEDULERS SHARE INFORMATION REGARDING THE SHOPPERS IN THEIR DATABASE?

The schedulers often work together and might recommend particular shoppers that have proven themselves by consistently turning in good reports on time.

DID YOU KNOW?

CUSTOMER SERVICE

The following are excerpts from two of shopping psychologist Paco Underhill's popular books. His company, Envirosell, has offices throughout the world.

> *We all enjoy the experience of good customer service. Add a clean store, organized merchandise, clearly marked prices, and quick service and chances are you'll return.*

> *Bad customer service is the #1 reason for non-repeat business.*

> *It costs five times more to attract a new customer than it does to retain an existing one.*

> *One out of three businesses fail because of employee theft.*

> *Sales experience is using our senses—sight, touch, smell, taste, hearing as the basis for choosing or rejecting something.*

> *The amount of time a shopper spends in a store depends on how comfortable and enjoyable the experience is. And, the longer a shopper remains in the store, the more he or she will buy.*

> *We may not enter a store if the line to pay looks too long or chaotic.*

> *We are spooked by too-close quarters.*

> *If we're made to wait too long, our impression of overall service plunges.*

> *A short wait enhances the entire shopping experience, a long one poisons it.*

> *Rude, distracted and intimidating service is the biggest deterrent to our returning."*

———————

" Underhill, Paco *Why We Buy: The Science of Shopping*. New York: Simon & Schuster

___ *How to Win Today's Retailing Wars*. 2001 and New York, Simon and Schuster

SALES KILLERS

The following are some good reasons a shopper might not return to a store.

He or she was unable to find someone to help them.

He or she couldn't pick up and feel the merchandise.

Boxes or obstacles were blocking the way.

The signs were too small.

The items were not priced, or were incorrectly priced.

The lighting was poor.

The salesperson was unresponsive.

Items were too low or too high to reach.

The line to pay was too long.

The shopping carts contained litter.

As a Mystery Shopper, your reports will reflect some of these dynamics. Was the line too long? Was the merchandise correctly priced? How long did you wait in line? How long before someone acknowledged you? When you asked a question was someone able to answer it?

Here again, as a Mystery Shopper, you will report on your experience. Your report will enable management to see where their problems are and take steps to fix them.

———————

"New Consumers are most stressed by...Narrow and congested aisles, Checkout Queues, Loud music..., Unhelpful staff, Trolley maneuverability,... Insufficient or ignorant staff"
  Lewis, David & Bridger, Darren 2000 *The Soul of the New Consumer*. London: Nicholas Breal

MYSTERY SHOPPING STATISTICS

- There are approximately one million Mystery Shoppers in the United States.

- Only ten percent of the shoppers are considered very good.

- Fifty percent of shops performed by Mystery Shoppers require follow up for missing information.

- One thousand shops were rejected by one company recently because the shoppers did not follow directions.

- Twenty five percent of applications by Mystery Shoppers are incomplete.

- Twenty five percent of accepted shops are not completed.

Can you do a better job?

Mystery Shopping companies are looking for you!

MYSTERY SHOPPING ANSWERS
SUCH QUESTIONS AS . . .

The following questions bear repeating. You will hear them over and over. Your reports will almost always include:

- ❖ How long did the customer wait before a salesperson greeted him or her?

- ❖ Did the greeting include a smile?

- ❖ Did the salesperson make eye contact?

- ❖ Was the salesperson able to answer your questions?

- ❖ Did the salesperson escort you to the product?

- ❖ Did the salesperson upsell, i.e., suggest an additional or complementary item?

Some of the shops you may be assigned will involve the situations mentioned above. For example, you may be assigned a Mystery Shop which requires you to enter a store and purchase a product.

Watch to see if the salesperson greets you within the timeframe set by the retailer. Does he or she answer your questions in a satisfactory manner? Does he or she offer an additional item? If the salesperson meets all of the criteria, then you may get to reward them with either a cash bonus or a reward certificate.

Sometimes you may not understand why you are asked to do a specific task. For instance you may be asked to report on how many cashier stations there were in a particular grocery store. Now you wonder to yourself—don't they know how many they have? Yes, they do know. But years ago, a grocery store manager added an additional cashier station in the store and pocketed the money. Without Mystery Shoppers it took years before corporate headquarters realized what was taking place. We may not always know why we're doing something, but there is usually a good reason and our job as Mystery Shoppers is to FOLLOW DIRECTIONS.

So many shops...
so little time...

2

APPLYING TO BECOME A MYSTERY SHOPPER

Applications will usually be submitted on the Mystery Shopping company website.

INITIAL APPLICATIONS

Your applications will usually be submitted on Mystery Shopping company websites. Below are some of the questions you should be prepared to answer.

Keep in mind that Mystery Shopping companies want you to be able to read and understand directions. If you do not complete the application completely and thoroughly, the companies will assume you will do the same with their reports and you will not be added to their database.

Have you done Mystery Shopping before?

You do not need to have experience as a Mystery Shopper. Most companies will hire you to work for them even if you have never been a Mystery Shopper before. Be honest and straightforward in your responses.

What companies have you worked for?

If you have had experience as a Mystery Shopper, you will be asked to list the companies you have worked with. Be sure to list only the Mystery Shopping companies and not the specific retailers or services which you shopped, as that information is, of course, confidential

Submit a paragraph on why they should hire you.

Normally you will be asked to write one paragraph about why you would make a good Mystery Shopper. Companies want to know whether or not you have report writing skills. Do you know how to spell? Do you know which words get capitalized? Where does a comma belong?

Write your own paragraph and review it to make sure it is 100% perfect. Then when you fill out applications you will have that one paragraph which you can use over and over again.

A sample paragraph follows this section

<u>Write one or two paragraphs about a recent experience at a restaurant or retail establishment.</u>

Here again you are being asked to show your writing skills. Keep in mind that <u>talking</u> about an experience and <u>writing</u> it down are two different matters. It takes practice to put your experience in writing so that a third person who wasn't with you, namely the editor, can read and understand exactly what happened. Try some practice writing. Think back to the last time you were in a store. Write it down and show it to someone. Can they picture exactly what happened without having to ask you questions? If so, you're on your way to a great career as a Mystery Shopper.

<u>What is your availability?</u>

It doesn't matter if you're working full time and only available on certain days. You will be notified of shops that match your availability. For example, if you say that you're available twenty four hours a day, seven days a week then when a shop comes up for a fast food restaurant at midnight, you will be notified and given the opportunity to apply for that shop. If you are only available on Saturdays, for instance, then you will be given notice of shops that can be done on Saturday.

<u>How far are you willing to travel?</u>

You will normally not be paid for mileage or reimbursed for your gas except in special circumstances. So when you answer the question about how far you are willing to travel, keep it in the range of your normal activities. If you never travel more than five miles from your home, put that down. If you travel a hundred miles a day round-trip to and from work, then you might want to put down a hundred miles.

<u>What is your Social Security Number?</u>

In these days of identity theft, this might be a cause of concern for those of you who are not willing to give out your Social Security Number. Keep in mind, however, that the Mystery Shopping company cannot hire you if you do not supply them with your Social Security Number. When you are on the company's website, look for the logo of a closed lock. This means that the website is secure. If you are still adamant about not revealing it, there is one solution I can offer. Since you will now be self employed, you can go to the Internal Revenue Service (IRS) and apply for an Employer Identification Number (EIN). You can then use that number instead of your Social Security Number. The IRS website is www.irs.gov.

What is your age? Ethnicity? Marital Status? Education? How many children do you have? Do you have pets? What is your income? Do you own your own home?

The Mystery Shopping company is not being nosey. The information you provide is put into their database so that shoppers in certain areas, or with special availability, etc., are notified when shops matching their specifications become available.

You will be asked many personal questions. Don't take offense or think that they are using this information as a way of excluding you. Actually, it's a way to include you in special shops when they have specific requirements for a client.

For example, a Mystery Shopping company may not wish to send a seventy year old woman to a sports bar or a twenty one year old to visit a senior housing development. As a Mystery Shopper you need to blend in and not be noticed. Fill out these personal questions to the best of your ability so that you will always be doing shops where you are most comfortable.

Do you have a computer?

When I first started shopping over twenty five years ago, we used mail and phones as a way to gather information and provide reports to the Mystery Shopping companies. When the fax machine became a popular home office tool, we advanced to that level. Now, of course, with the popularity of personal computers, they have become the most commonly used communication method employed by the Mystery Shopping companies. While a few companies still do use the phone and fax, most Mystery Shopping companies will require that you have access to a computer.

Libraries, schools and internet cafes can help you get started if you are not yet connected to the world wide cyberspace web. I strongly urge everyone to take advantage of this fantastic technology for use not only as a Mystery Shopper, but also as an added way of communication and information gathering for the Twenty First Century. There are classes being offered (many at no charge) in virtually every city and state.

What is your skill level?

How proficient are you with your computer? Some of the forms you will be given require very little skill; some require more challenging skill levels. The Mystery Shopping company wants to be sure they are offering you assignments that you will be able to successfully complete.

Do you have a laptop computer?

Occasionally shops come up that require portability and instant feedback. If you have a laptop computer, you will be eligible for those shops.

Do you have a scanner?

You will need to submit your receipts. In many cases you can send in the receipts by fax, mail, or by scanning them onto your computer. Some Mystery Shopping companies are now requiring that all the receipts be scanned.

Do you have a digital camera?

Some shops require the use of a digital camera. You may take a picture of an item or a location and then immediately download it together with your report to the Mystery Shopping company.

Do you have access to email?

This is by far the most common and the easiest way for the schedulers to contact you. You will be asked to provide your email address. Be sure your internet service provider (ISP) and your software will allow your email address to receive email attachments.

Do you have a printer?

You will need to print out your instructions and evaluation forms.

What type of computer programs do you have?

You will receive your assignments in many different formats. Sometimes they will be on the company's website and you will need to print them out. Sometimes they will come in your email as an attachment. Some of the forms may come as a Word or Excel attachment. Can your computer accept those types of assignments?

You do not have to have all of this equipment to start out with. The more equipment you have, the more types of assignments you can accept. Start out slowly and then as you see that you are enjoying this work as a Mystery Shopper, you can gradually add to your equipment.

Will you accept payments via Paypal?

Paypal is an online bank that many of the Mystery Shopping companies use to pay you. Paypal is part of eBay. It is very easy to open a free account at Paypal. Go to their website www.paypal.com and read about them. When you are ready to open an account, you will be able to say 'YES" when you fill out applications at Mystery Shopping companies and they ask whether or not you will accept payments via Paypal.

There are several different types of accounts offered by Paypal. My suggestion would be to open a Personal Account or a Premier Account. Do not open a Business Account at this time as there are likely to be additional charges for your transactions.

What about Gold or Silver Certification?

In 2002 the Mystery Shoppers Providers Association held a special conference in Nashville, Tennessee. Their goal was to raise the standard of reporting and improve the performance of Mystery Shoppers on behalf of the Association's members, clients and associates.

I attended this workshop and found it to be an informative event. There were opportunities to meet with the owners of Mystery Shopping companies throughout the world, and to have one on one conversation with the schedulers and editors. Mystery Shoppers who attended this workshop were awarded with Gold Certification. (The cost was $99.)

The Association now offers this workshop throughout the country and provides an opportunity for Mystery Shoppers to get together, gain insight and tips about the current programs and practices in the field, and receive Gold Certification. You can also receive Gold Certification through their Gold DVD which includes the same content as the live workshops. Whether you choose the live workshop or the DVD, the cost is $99. The DVD also has a $5 mailing cost added for a total of $104.

Note: In order to receive the Gold Certification, you must first take a brief online test (for which there is a charge) and become Silver Certified. Once Silver Certified, you are eligible to become Gold Certified

You can find out more about the certification programs by visiting the Mystery Shopping Providers Association (MSPA) website. As stated on their website, *Two certification programs are offered by the industry association, Mystery Shopping Providers Association. Participation is open to any independent contractor interested in learning more about industry standards and the skills involved in customer service evaluations. Certification is not required by the association.* The association also states that some companies in their organization may give preference to Gold Certified shoppers. (Note: In my personal experience, even without certification you may also be given preference for assignments once you have shown a company that you are dependable and can follow their directions. Additionally, only a small percentage of mystery shopping companies use this certification method.)

The association also offers a Shoppers Workshop. This does not provide any certification for attending.

You do not need to be certified to do most Mystery Shopping. It is your decision. Additionally, several other associations offer certification. If you decide to become certified, I would recommend MSPA.
Their web address is www.mysteryshop.org/shoppers.

WOULD YOU MAKE A GOOD MYSTERY SHOPPER?

Practice Exercise

Why should the Mystery Shopping company hire you?

SAMPLE

I am confident that I would make a good Mystery Shopper for your company because I understand the importance of good customer service. I enjoy interacting with the public and I write well. You can depend on me to follow your guidelines in preparing objective and complete reports. I have a background in business administration and teaching. I am conscientious, dependable, and my work schedule is flexible.

WRITE YOUR OWN PARAGRAPH BELOW (100 words or less)

YOUR OWN WRITING SAMPLES

Practice Exercise

Write one or two paragraphs about a recent experience you had in a retail setting. Stick to the facts and remember that an editor has to feel as if he or she was right there with you.

3

WRITING REPORTS

*You must be able to read
and
understand directions.*

IMPORTANT TIPS

BE SPECIFIC

Being vague in your reports can be a major problem for your editor. You need to be detailed when you prepare your evaluations. If you write on your report that "the floor was dirty," that does not give enough information to the store owners. You need to include the specifics such as, "The carpet had three large stains," or "The floors were polished but had litter under most of the tables," or "The tile was sticky from spilled drinks."

COMMITMENTS

If you make a commitment to do a shop, you must follow through. If you do not complete your assignment, your name will be taken off of the database and you will not be used again. Although companies understand that emergencies happen to all of us, a Mystery Shopper with too many emergencies causes problems for the scheduling department and they are not likely to use you in the future. Remember, if you are offered an assignment, you do not have to accept it. But once you accept it, the client and staff are depending on you to follow through.

READ AND UNDERSTAND THE DIRECTIONS

Every business has its own set of requirements, challenges and needs for specific information. You must read and understand the guidelines they furnish to know what these requirements are for each report. If you do not understand something, ask the scheduler. They are there to help you and they want you to succeed in doing a good job.

REPORT WRITING POINTERS

- ❖ Write your reports in past tense
- ❖ Do not use slang.
- ❖ Do not use contractions.
- ❖ Do not give estimated times. Be exact.
- ❖ Be consistent
- ❖ Proofread your work.
- ❖ Tell the story.
- ❖ Avoid phrases like "it seemed," "it appeared to be"

NARRATIVE SAMPLE
(excerpt)

Here is an excerpt from a recent narration for a restaurant assignment. You will notice that the report sticks to the facts and makes no judgments.

At 6:57 p.m., the hostess, Christine, escorted us to our table. She walked at a very fast pace and did not warn us about the set of steps just past the hostess station. After we were seated she handed us our menus and said, "Enjoy."

The busser, Joseph, came by at 7:00 p.m. and brought us water. He did not smile or make eye contact.

Jackie, our female server, came by at 7:01 p.m. and asked if she could start us off with a drink. We asked if she could recommend a wine for us and she pointed to the wine list on the table, telling us that all of the wines were listed in the menu. We ordered the Gewurtztraminer and she started to leave, saying she would bring us a glass. We told her we would like a bottle.

She returned two minutes later with the bottle of wine. She showed us the label and repeated the name. The bottle was nicely chilled. She uncorked it and presented a small portion to my partner. As soon as he gave his approval, she poured a glass for me and an additional amount for my partner. She set the wine on the table with its label facing us.

She asked if we were ready to order and told us that the soup special was chicken and wild rice. We ordered an appetizer and our entrees at 7:07 p.m. ...

DIFFERENT WRITING STYLES

When you are writing a report as a Mystery Shopper your focus should be on providing clear and accurate details of your experience. The editors are not looking for a restaurant critique or a novel. Here are some examples...

NOVEL

It was a dark and stormy night and the wind blew angrily, causing trees to sway and eerie sounds to resonate through our senses. We felt an a air of apprehension as we came upon the dark door that was swinging on its hinges warning of dangers that may lie ahead....Inside the aroma of barbecued meats filled our hearts with longing and our taste buds with joy. We were served heaping platters of appetizers that piqued our very souls and made us cry out for more.

RESTAURANT CRITIQUE

The ambiance of the restaurant was reminiscent of King Arthur's Roundtable. Although dimly lit, the décor was tasteful and the heavy furniture was comfortable. We were offered a variety of food which was more bountiful than distinguished. The food was ill prepared and tasted like leftovers from the original banquet.

EXCERPTS FROM A MYSTERY SHOPPER REPORT

We arrived at 7 p.m. It was raining heavily and a strong wind kept the front door from securely closing. We were seated within two minutes of our arrival and Jennie, our server, greeted us one minute later. She brought us a large tray of hot appetizers to enjoy while we made our dinner selection. There were four items on the platter which were attractively displayed. The barbecue chicken wings were meaty and tender. They were served with a tangy sauce that was rich and thick...

MAKE YOUR OWN THESAURUS

A Thesaurus is a good investment. You will refer to it often. Prepare your own additions and keep them handy. This will help you with describing what happened. Here are some words to get you started. Add to the list, be creative.

POSITIVE WORDS

appealing, attentive, attractive, beautiful, bright, charming, considerate, delicious, delightful, energetic, enchanting, engaging, enthusiastic, exciting, flavorful, fragrant, friendly, fresh, graceful, immaculate, impressive, informative, knowledgeable, lovely, mouth-watering, orderly, pleasing, polite, pretty, professional, smooth, sparkling, thoughtful, tidy, tranquil, welcoming, well-seasoned

NEGATIVE WORDS

apathetic, bored, chaotic, confusing, cramped, crowded, dark, disarray, dingy, discourteous, disorganized, distasteful, distracted, dirty, dusty, grimy, hurried, indifferent, insensitive, monotone, mumbled, nasty, offensive, preoccupied, rehearsed, rude, smelly, sour, thoughtless, tired, turmoil, unconcerned, unkempt, unkind, withdrawn

ACTION WORDS

described, directed, discussed, encouraged, explained, focused, furnished, guided, informed, initiated, offered, praised, presented, promoted, provided, recommended, referred, responded, upsold

FOOD DESCRIPTIONS

Al dente, charbroiled, chilled, creamy, crisp, crunchy, deep fried, delicate flavor, drizzled with, firm texture, fresh, garnished with, golden brown, hint of garlic, julienne, light, smoky, piping hot, pungent, pureed, rich, seared, slight bitterness, smooth, soft, spicy, sweet, tender, topped with, vibrant

COMPLETE THE PHRASES

Practice Exercise

Try some of these writing exercises. At first it may be difficult for you to complete the sentences, but the more you practice writing, the easier the words will flow. The next page will show you some examples.

Think back to your last visit to a restaurant or retail store.

The salesperson was_____

He/she greeted me by saying_____

The appetizers were_____

The merchandise was_____

The ambiance was_____ _____

The entrance was_____

The server said_____

We enjoyed the_____

The service was_____

I would return because_____

COMPLETED PHRASES

Examples

The sales person was friendly and helpful. She answered my questions and escorted me to the product I was looking for.

He greeted my by saying, "Good afternoon. Welcome to the Sunshine Spa."

The appetizers were attractively served on a large 14" oval platter. The quesadillas were cut into four wedges and surrounded by a green leafy lettuce garnish. The tortillas were golden brown and oozing with cheese and spices.

The merchandise was organized and attractively displayed, showing each of the colors that were available.

The ambiance was warm and comfortable. The tables were set with crisp, white linen and shiny glasses. Candles were glowing on each table and the lights were appropriately dimmed, adding a touch of romance.

The entrance was cluttered and confusing. Several boxes were next to the entry way and I did not know which way to turn once I entered.

The server said, "Good evening. My name is Helen and I will be your server this evening. Can I start you off with some wine or a cocktail from the bar?"

We enjoyed the colorful displays and bright signs. It was easy to identify the various items and choose accordingly.

He suggested the Chocolate Delight and the Key Lime Pie, assuring us that they were the most popular items.

The service was slow and we were not able to catch our server's attention. He was busy with a large group in another room and his attention was more focused on their needs.

We would return because the food was prepared exactly to our specifications. The taste was excellent and the setting was elegant.

BASIC INFORMATION FOR RESTAURANT REPORTS

Focus on the following issues when you are ready to write your restaurant evaluations. These issues are explained further on the following page.

GREETER

> How were you greeted?
> Were you seated promptly?

SERVER

> Salesmanship
> Attentiveness
> Attitude
> Timeliness

FOOD PRESENTATION

> How was it presented?
> Would you order it again?

TEAMWORK

> Was there a team spirit among employees?

MANAGER

> What was the manager doing?

BASIC RESTAURANT REPORTS

Explained

Every report you do will have different questions. Some reports may ask you to remember specific quotes; others may not think that is necessary. Sometimes a company will ask you to refer to the Employees as Associates, or Team Members. Some instructions may ask you to refer to employees by name only, and then some may ask you to be general in your descriptions and not to refer to them by name.

GREETER

Did the greeter say hello? What was the actual greeting?

Were you seated promptly? If you were told that there was a thirty minute wait, were you seated within the thirty minutes? It's perfectly acceptable to have to wait but it is not acceptable to be told that the wait is thirty minutes and then have to wait for one hour.

SERVER

How did the server greet you? Did the server suggest specific items? The servers are salespeople. They might do one of these three things after they greet you. They may say 1. "Are you ready to order?" 2. "Do you want a drink?" 3. "Would you like to try one of our Margaritas? We make the best Margaritas in town and tonight we're having a special." If they offer 1 or 2 they are not salespeople. They are just order takers. They should be suggesting specific items for you.

How attentive was your server? Did they offer to refill your glasses when they were almost empty? Did they bring you more bread when your basket was empty?

Were they friendly? Did they have a bad day and take it out on you? Or did they make your visit more enjoyable?

How timely was your food service? You will be given specific guidelines about how long it should take for you to receive each different service; the appetizer, the entrée, the dessert, etc. Was your food delivered within those timelines?

FOOD PRESENTATION

How was it presented? The server or food runner should know which of you ordered which particular item and it should be set in front of you and announced.

Explain whether or not you would order that item again. You will need to say why you would or would not.

TEAMWORK

Did all of the employees work together as a team? Did they help one another? If you needed something and asked another server, did they accommodate you?

Once while at an upscale restaurant, our appetizers were delivered by a food expeditor. We pointed out that we did not have any silverware. He said, "Ill tell your server." This was not teamwork. The story does not end there because he never informed our server and we eventually walked over to the next table and helped ourselves to the silverware.

MANAGER

There is usually a manager on duty. Did you see what the manager was doing? Comment on their involvement. Were they greeting guests, interacting with employees, visiting tables?

BASIC INFORMATION FOR RETAIL REPORTS

Focus on the following concerns when you are ready to write your retail evaluations. These issues are explained further on the following page.

ORGANIZATION

Were the shelves free from dust?
Were products organized?
Were the aisles clear?
Were items priced in a professional manner?

TIMELINESS

How long before you were greeted?
Were you greeted AND offered assistance?

FRIENDLINESS

Did the associates smile and make eye contact?

KNOWLEDGE

Were the associates able to answer your questions?

SALES ABILITY

Did an associate offer to escort you?
Did an associate point out positive features?

CASHIER

Was your order processed in a timely manner?
How long did you wait in line?

UPSELL

Were additional matching or complementary items suggested?

BASIC RETAIL REPORTS

Explained

Although the following are the types of questions you might find in a typical retail evaluation form, some retailers are more focused on customer service than others. Sometimes you may perform an evaluation on a retail store that only involves the aspect of cleanliness, or perhaps the employee awareness. For instance, I was once asked to purchase a pair of shoes and instructed to put two different sizes in the box. This was to see if the employee would check the inside of the box. Yes, they did get it right!

ORGANIZATION

Look around. Are the shelves dusty? Are the items dirty and old looking? Were the sizes or styles organized so that you could easily locate what you were looking for? Were the items priced? Were they correctly priced?

TIMELINESS

How long before someone greeted you? How long before you were offered assistance. Some stores require that their employees greet you within two minutes. Keep in mind that a greeting and an offer to assist are two different things. It may not be not acceptable for an employee to merely say, "Can I help you?" They should first greet you in a friendly manner by saying "Hello" or some similar greeting.

FRIENDLINESS

What were the attitudes of the employees? Were they cheerful and friendly?

KNOWLEDGE

You should ask an "open-ended" question. How did they respond? If they did not know the answer, did they try to find out for you? Avoid questions that they may answer by saying YES or NO without an explanation. For example, instead of saying, "Does it come with a warranty?" you would ask, "How long is the warranty?"

SALES ABILITY

When you asked about a product, did the salesperson escort you? Or did they point? How did they respond? Were they able to discuss the product, make recommendations, and show you the features?

CASHIER

Did you have to wait in line to pay for your purchase? How long did you wait? Did the cashier greet you? What was the greeting? What was the closing or parting comment?

UPSELL

Did the salesperson or cashier offer any additional items? Invite you to return? What was the closing remark?

Upselling goes straight to the retailer's bottom line and can affect an employee's direct compensation. It even affects executive bonuses which may be tied directly to profitable performance. Upselling is like finding money.

When you go into a retail store, you want to give the employees a chance to do their best sales job. Allow them every opportunity. Rather than asking for a specific item, you might be hesitant and see if they can suggest something. Ask questions, have an objection and see if they can overcome the objection. Let them sell you and hopefully they'll do a superb job and you can write up a glowing report. After all, that's what Mystery Shop reporting is all about.

GOOD WRITING EXAMPLES

SOME EXAMPLES OF
HELPFUL WRITTEN REMARKS

"Sally went out of her way to find us a booth near the window as we requested."

"Helen explained the features and benefits thoroughly, adding the information that we would receive an additional discount if we bought both of the items she presented."

"The restaurant was beautifully decorated with a Mexican theme and we felt as if we were dining at a beach cantina in Acapulco."

"The associate continued to focus on her paperwork while I asked questions. She did not look at me or make eye contact."

"Caroline, the greeter, opened the door for us when we arrived and smiled warmly as she said, 'Welcome.'"

"The steak was tender and juicy with a tangy Béarnaise sauce which enhanced its flavor."

"As we departed the restaurant, the cashier smiled and wished us a pleasant evening inviting us to return."

"Fred stood up from his desk to greet me, shook my hand, and offered me his business card."

You will notice that specific details are given. This is helpful information for the business owner. It was good to know that the steak was tender and juicy. When management gets another Mystery Shopping report that says the steak was tough and dry, the managers will know that there is a specific problem in the kitchen that needs to be dealt with, thanks to you, the Mystery Shopper.

POOR WRITING EXAMPLES

Practice Exercise

HOW WOULD YOU IMPROVE THE SENTENCES BELOW?
Remember that you need to be specific when writing a report.

For example, instead of saying that the floor was dirty you would note why it was dirty. Was there litter on the floor? Describe the specific things which led to your judgment. Did the carpeting have several unsightly stains or tears?

1) The floor was dirty.

2) The store was understaffed.

3) The temperature in the store seemed cold.

4) They should have offered a beverage.

5) Last time I was here they were more helpful.

6) I don't like French fries.

7) The cashier looked unprofessional.

8) The meat tasted funny.

9) We received our entrees in about 10 or 12 minutes.

10) The restaurant was clean.

CORRECTING
POOR WRITING EXAMPLES

1) The floor was dirty.
   BE SPECIFIC
   The carpet had three large stains and litter under several tables including our table.

2) The store was understaffed.
   REPORT FACTS. DON'T COME TO YOUR OWN CONCLUSIONS
   There was one employee and ten customers were in line. I waited eighteen minutes for service.

3) The temperature in the store seemed cold.
   AVOID WORDS LIKE "SEEMED" OR "APPEARED TO BE"
   It was cold in the store.   Several customers were observed putting on their jackets.

4) They should have offered a beverage.
   DON'T TELL THEM WHAT TO DO.
   I was not offered a beverage.

5) Last time I was here they were more helpful.
   DON'T COMPARE SHOPS. TREAT EACH ONE AS A NEW EXPERIENCE
   The staff was busy stocking the shelves and they were not responsive to my questions.

6) I don't like French fries.
   DON'T TAKE AN ASSIGNMENT IF YOU DON'T LIKE THE PRODUCT
   The French fries were limp and greasy.

7) The cashier looked unprofessional.
   BE SPECIFIC
   The cashier wore a stained blouse with several buttons missing.

8) The meat tasted funny.
  BE SPECIFIC
  The meat was dry and had a foul odor.

9) We received our entrees in about 10 or 12 minutes.
  EXACT TIMINGS ARE REQUIRED
  We received our entrees in 11 minutes and 32 seconds.

10) The restaurant was clean.
  BE SPECIFIC
  The floors and carpets were freshly vacuumed and the counter tops were shining with no streaks or food residue.

It is a great feeling of accomplishment when you return to a specific location and discover that a problem you noted in your report was corrected.

We once visited a restaurant at five o'clock pm for dinner and thought the restaurant was closed because it looked dark. We tried the door and discovered that the restaurant was actually open. This information was noted in my report. The following month when we returned, a large neon OPEN sign was displayed in the window.

Another time I had an assignment at a grocery chain and they had a policy that no more than three shopping carts could be loose in the parking lot at any one time. In my report I stated that the carts were indeed, put into their stalls, however, the employees were in such a hurry to put them away that they did not clean the left-over papers and debris that was left in the carts. The following month and every time thereafter, I have observed that the carts are put away AND clean.

Remember, your reports have impact!

Work from home...
Set your own schedule...

4

UNDERSTANDING GUIDELINES

*Guidelines are the instructions
you will receive when you
have been offered a
Mystery Shopping assignment.*

GENERAL GUIDELINES

Once you have been assigned a shop you will be given specific guidelines. Make sure you understand what it is you are to do. Contact your scheduler if there is anything about which you are not certain.

Be sure to review your guidelines immediately. Don't wait until the last minute. You may run into problems that could easily have been solved if you were properly prepared.

GUIDELINES VS. EVALUATION FORMS

GUIDELINES are the particular instructions you will receive after you have been assigned to a particular shop.

EVALUATION forms are the forms you will fill out after you have completed the assignment. These forms will be completed by you and sent directly to the Mystery Shopping company through their website, as an email attachment, or in such other form that the Mystery Shopping company may request.

In addition to reviewing the guidelines, it is also a good idea to review the evaluation forms. Many times you will find that the evaluation forms contain additional, helpful information. Review both forms at least two times; once when you receive the assignment and then again just prior to going on the shop.

GUIDELINE HINTS

Read the directions carefully and make a list of anything that you might not understand. Contact your scheduler with questions before you go on the shop. The scheduler is available to help you. They want you to do a good job, so do not hesitate to ask about anything you might not understand.

For instance, if you were told to watch for "auctioning of food" while at a restaurant, would you understand what that meant? Auctioning occurs when your food is delivered and you are asked, "Who ordered the steak? Who's got the chicken?"

Another example of a question you might not understand is, "How many people were in line?" Does that include everyone in line or just the paying customer? Does that include you? If the instructions say you've been assigned a dinner shop between 6:00 and 8:00 p.m., does that mean you have to arrive before 8:00, be seated before 8:00, or be finished eating by 8:00? Your specific guidelines will clarify these matters.

It is to your advantage to read the guidelines carefully and be sure to clear up anything that might be misunderstood. Once you're on the actual assignment, it's probably too late to wonder what to do.

When you are given an assignment, keep in mind that you are not there to create or initiate problems but to report accurately what you observe while remaining as inconspicuous as possible.

If you go into a retail store, give the salesperson every opportunity to do the job they were trained for. You might go into a gift store and rather than say, "Show me a Monopoly set," you might say, "I'm looking for a gift for a ten year old. Watch to see how the salesperson handles your request. Do they ask questions, do they escort you to some products, and do they explain how the products work? Let the salesperson do their job and hopefully they'll be a shining star and you can write a dazzling report. If you don't give them the opportunity to offer great service, you'll never know what they could have done.

Prepare in advance for the role you will play. Dress and act the part. If you are going into a fast food restaurant you can dress more casually than if you were going into a bank. If your guidelines tell you to pretend to be looking for a 4,000 square foot home in the million dollar range, then you will certainly dress the part. Then again, you may be assigned a shop at an apartment complex that offers government assistance. You would not want to drive to that location in your new BMW.

GENERAL GUIDELINES

Sample

ABC MYSTERY SHOPPING COMPANY

NAME_____SHOPPER #_____

Please review this form before you complete the shop. If you have any questions, please call or email our coordinator, Mrs. Jones.

1. You have been assigned_____ (store and location)

2. Assignment #_____

3. Please verify this location before you complete your shop.

4. This assignment must be completed on _____ (specific date or date range)

5. Your compensation for this shop will be _____plus reimbursement of _____

6. You must confirm receipt and acceptance of this assignment within 48 hours by logging in to our website.

7. You will be evaluating service and cleanliness during your visit.

8. The evaluation must be turned in within 24 hours after you have completed your assignment.

9. Your receipt must be sent within 48 hours after completion via fax, scanning, or mail.

FAILURE TO COMPLETE THE ASSIGNMENT WITHIN OUR TIME LIMITS WILL RESULT IN NON-PAYMENT FOR THIS SHOP.

Our guidelines change monthly. Please be sure you follow the specific requirements on the following page for this month's assignment.

1. The departments to visit for this evaluation are: _____

2. Portray yourself as an average customer. Do not let anyone see you taking notes.

3. Record the time of entry and the time you departed. You MUST stay a minimum of _____ minutes in the store.

4. If you are not assisted within 5 minutes, you MUST seek an employee to assist you.

5. Be sure to ask at least one question and enter their response.

6. You MUST get the name of the salesperson who assisted you.

7. You MUST try to get the name of all other employees that you come in contact with. If you cannot get their name, we need a description, including gender, age, height, hair color and style.

8. You MUST make a purchase.

9. You MUST visit the restroom.

10. You MUST submit the itemized receipt. You will not be reimbursed without the receipt.

11. Record how long it took for your transaction from the time you entered the line to pay until you were handed your receipt.

12. Explain in detail any "No" answers.

13. Every question must be answered for your shop to be valid.

14. Write a minimum of two paragraphs explaining your experience.

15. Do not carry your evaluation form into the store with you.

16. Complete your evaluation immediately after leaving the store parking area.

17. Do not reveal that you are a Mystery Shopper.

18. Keep your paperwork until you are paid for the shop.

Let's see, was that shop lunch on Saturday or brunch on Sunday?

5

SAMPLE EVALUATIONS AND ASSIGNMENTS

Every assignment will have a unique set of instructions.

EACH ASSIGNMENT
WILL BE DIFFERENT

The following pages will show you additional types of forms that may be used. Sometimes your forms will be very easy and take you just a few minutes to complete.

At the other extreme you might be asked to write long narratives that will take you anywhere from one to several hours to complete. You will have the option of deciding which companies you want to work with and you will be able to choose between those assignments that require long narratives or simple forms.

Many times you will be asked to write two or three sentences in answer to each question. Keep in mind that you must always adhere to the guidelines. You can never write less than what the instructions require. For instance, if the guidelines say to write three sentences, you cannot write two sentences. However, you can usually write more. Remember: More is often acceptable – less is unacceptable.

When you are asked a YES or NO question and are not quite sure how to answer it, my suggestion would be to answer NO and then in the narrative section of your report, explain why you said NO. For instance, if a questionnaire asks if the employees were wearing nametags and nine of the ten employees wore nametags—you would answer the question NO. That is because they were not all wearing nametags. Then in the narrative part you would indicate that nine employees wore nametags and one employee did not.

If you are asked to score something on a scale of one to ten, use your best judgment. Don't ask someone else to help you make up your mind. The Mystery Shopping company has hired you and they are interested in your observations.

You have a lot of responsibility and everyone; the Mystery Shopping company, the individual business, the scheduler, and the editor are depending on you to provide a thorough and honest evaluation.

Always give the employee the benefit of the doubt if you are uncertain about a particular action. For instance, if you don't remember whether or not they smiled at you, do not say that they did not smile.

PRACTICE YOUR SKILLS

It is a good idea to review some typical types of assignments before you actually go out on your very first job. Following are some sample evaluation forms. Practice your skills by reviewing the forms before going on your normal shopping visits. When you return, see how accurately you can furnish the information requested.

The very first actual assignment you have will be a challenge but if you practice beforehand, it will be easier for you.

You can never take the paperwork into the store with you, but you can jot down a few notes and keep them in your pocket to help you remember.

Most things are easy to remember. You will remember the taste of the last meal you had. You will remember whether or not the bank lobby was clean. You will remember whether or not you were greeted.

Think back to your last visit at a retail store. Can you remember what happened?

You may not remember whether the music was playing, if there were any hand-written signs, or if there were two or three cashiers. However, if you know before going in that you must look for those things, you will start becoming more and more aware and soon it will become automatic.

The two things that most new shoppers will have the hardest time remembering are exact times and employee names.

HELPFUL HINTS

NAMES AND DESCRIPTIONS

Keep in mind that each Mystery Shopping company and each retail store has its own method and their instructions may vary for every single shop you do. Sometimes you will be told YOU MUST GET THEIR NAMES and sometimes the instructions will say TRY TO GET THEIR NAMES. Remember that if you MUST, you absolutely MUST. You may risk not being paid for that shop if you don't comply with those requirements. Sometimes your instructions will tell you to try to get their names and say that it is okay to ask the employee for their name. Other companies might tell you never to ask the employee for their name.

This may sound repetitive, but I can't stress enough how important it is that you READ AND UNDERSTAND THE DIRECTIONS.

If it is okay to ask their name, you can do so by simply asking for their name and then following it up with a comment or a question. You certainly wouldn't want to ask their name and just walk away.

Once, while on an assignment I asked the employee why he was the only employee in the store that day not wearing a nametag. He said, "In case a Mystery Shopper comes in, they won't know who I am." I, of course, followed up by asking, "What is a Mystery Shopper?"

Another way to get the name is to ask someone else. For instance, you might say to your server, "The manager over there looks familiar. I think I went to school with him. Is his name Bob?" The server will then usually say, "No, his name is Fred."

Descriptions are also important. Many times you will only be asked whether they were male or female and the color and style of their hair. However, some companies want a full description. Be considerate when describing someone and never write down anything that would be hurtful.

RECORDING ACCURATE TIMES

This is perhaps the most difficult part of any assignment. Sometimes you are asked to record times in minutes and seconds. Wear a watch with large numbers and a second hand. Or, carry a stop watch with you. Be prepared.

Many of us now have our own Palm Pilots and cell phones. These are easy instruments to use to record times. So many people use them now that it may not be noticeable if you enter some information. But, be cautious.

If you're at a casual restaurant, a cell phone is a handy way to record times. Pretend you're making a phone call. Your cell phone will remember at least the last 10 sets of numbers you put in, so when you leave the restaurant, you will also have the correct timings. Some phones will only remember the numbers if you hit send, but you can always enter a number into memory and even add alpha characters for a description or label. But be sure to read your guidelines carefully. Some instructions may direct that you do not use a cell phone. At a Five Star restaurant it would never be acceptable to use a cell phone in the dining area.

TAKING NOTES

You will NEVER take your paper work into the store with you. You might want to plan on visiting the rest room a few times while you are on an assignment. I usually keep a small notebook in my pocket and then jot down some items while I'm in the restroom to help me remember when I get home. You can also devise other ways to take notes. But, be careful as many veteran employees are wise to our tricks and you may be spotted.

What happens if you get spotted? Your report will not be used and you will not be paid. So please be discreet.

If the Mystery Shopping company which assigned you the shop has no objections, you can try any of the following: If you're in a grocery store, many people carry a shopping list, so you can also carry a shopping list and fill in notes within your shopping list. If you're by yourself at a restaurant, you can do a crossword puzzle. No one looks to see what you've actually written in all those little squares. Or, if you and a guest are having lunch, why not pretend it's a business meeting and talk about your plans for the coming advertising promotion, or some other business topic while you actually will be writing down some important items to help you remember. My husband and I often keep a real estate booklet with us and talk about the new houses. I might discuss our color scheme and the floor plan and pretend to be placing furniture on the booklet while I'm writing down key words to help me remember everything later.

As soon as you have finished with your assignment and leave the site, drive your car to a nearby parking lot, and write everything down while it is still fresh in your mind.

SCHEDULING YOUR ASSIGNMENTS

Scheduling is a difficult and challenging aspect of your shopping career.

Keep in mind that you do not have to accept every assignment that is offered to you. But, once you have accepted an assignment you must make every effort possible to stand by your commitment. If you let the company down, they will not likely use you again.

Keep a calendar and be sure you list your assignments carefully. Sometimes you are given a span of several days to complete the assignment. Sometimes you are given a specific date and even a specific time. Make sure that you have saved the time to be able to perform that assignment.

Also, make sure that you have factored in the time allotted for you to send in your completed report. On the average, you have twenty four hours to complete and submit the evaluation. However, I have seen shops that allowed only twelve hours, and some that permitted only four hours. You can do the best shop in the world, but if you fail to return the evaluation within the time guidelines, you will not be paid.

TAKING CHILDREN ON ASSIGNMENTS

It may not always be wise to take children on assignments. You are there to do a job and children are sometimes a distraction. It is not always fair to the employee that you are evaluating as sometimes they may be more focused on your "cute" child and fall short on their sales performance. There are, of course, some assignments where children would be welcome. For instance, a casual restaurant that caters to children by offering crayons, etc. Or perhaps a children's clothing store. I saw an assignment recently where it asked for a child under 10 to try on a pair of children's shoes. Read your instructions carefully and if in doubt about whether or not to bring your child, check with the scheduler.

SAMPLE EVALUATIONS

All of the Mystery Shopping companies have their own styling formats, which are often dictated by their clients. I have included many different types of forms to give you an idea of the diversity you might expect. It's challenging and interesting to learn the different evaluation methods.

SAMPLE EVALUATION

BANK

SHOPPER: DATE:

BANK/BRANCH:

TIME ARRIVED: TIME DEPARTED:

NAME OF TELLER:

NAME OF NEW ACCOUNT REPRESENTATIVE:

THIS MONTH'S SCENARIO

1. Teller. Conduct a teller transaction (purchase or cash a Traveler's Check). Report on length of wait and friendliness of teller. Did the teller smile, give you their undivided attention, thank you?

2. Customer Service Representative (CSR). Inquire about a new account (You have just moved to the city.) Report on knowledge of employee and friendliness. Did they answer your questions, mention other products, and offer their business card?

WRITE A MINIMUM OF THREE PARAGRAPHS

The first paragraph will be your initial impressions on the condition of the exterior and interior of the branch.

In the second paragraph, include the amount of time you waited in line, how the teller greeted you, if he/she was focused on your transaction, and what their exit greeting was.

In the third paragraph, include the amount of time you waited before seeing a CSR, did they stand up and shake your hand, did they introduce themselves and offer you a seat. What was discussed? Please be detailed and include actual quotes when possible.

PLEASE CIRCLE THE APPROPRIATE ANSWER

EXTERIOR CONDITION	EXCELLENT	GOOD	FAIR
INTERIOR LOBBY	EXCELLENT	GOOD	FAIR
TELLER	EXCELLENT	GOOD	FAIR
CSR	EXCELLENT	GOOD	FAIR

SAMPLE EVALUATION

FAST FOOD/RESTAURANT

ASSIGNED TO_____
RESTAURANT _____
ADDRESS_____ _____
DATE_____TIME IN_____TIME OUT_____
AMOUNT SPENT_____
CASHIER NAME OR DESCRIPTION_____

ENTRY
Was the exterior clean and inviting?   Y   N
Was the landscaping trim and attractive?   Y   N
Were the windows and doors clean?   Y   N

DINING ROOM
Was the dining area clean (carpets/blinds, etc)?   Y   N
Were there any unbussed tables?   Y   N
If so, how many?   _____

SERVICE
How many customers were in front of you?   _____
How long from the time you entered the line
  until you placed your order (minutes and seconds)?   _____
How long until you received your order?   _____
Did the cashier smile and make eye contact?   Y   N
Was your order correct?   Y   N

FOOD QUALITY
What did you order? _____
Describe the quality of the food (three sentences minimum)

RESTROOM
Was the restroom clean and fully supplied?   Y   N

SUMMARY
Based on your experience, how often would you return?

Would you recommend this location to your friends?   Y   N
Why or why not? _____

Write a minimum of two paragraphs regarding your experience.

SAMPLE EVALUATION

CASUAL RESTAURANT

Location:_____

Shopper ID #_____

Date shopped:_____

Time entered:_____

Time departed:_____

Check amount:_____

Tip amount:_____

Valet parking charge if any _____

Was the parking lot well lit and free of debris?   Y   N

Were signs posted regarding parking fees or tipping?   Y   N

Was the lobby area clean and inviting?   Y   N

How long did you wait for a table?   _____

How long before your server greeted you at the table?   _____

What did the server say?_____

What drinks were suggested?_____

Were you offered an appetizer?   Y   N

Was dessert suggested?   Y   N

How long from the time you ordered until received?

Drinks_____
Entrée_____
Dessert_____

Did the server check back within 2 minutes?   Y   N

Were your plates removed as you finished?   Y   N

Continued on next page

Were you offered refills?   Y   N

What did you order? _____

Describe presentation and taste. Rate on a scale of one to ten
with ten being the best. _____

_____

Did you see a manager? What was the manager doing? _____

_____

Name and description of
    Host_____

Name and description of
    Server_____

Name and description of
    Manager_____

Write a minimum of three paragraphs describing your experience.

_____

_____

_____

Would you return?
    Why?_____

SAMPLE EVALUATION

RETAIL

NAME_____DATE SHOPPED_____
STORE_____ADDRESS_____
TIME IN_____TIME OUT_____AMOUNT SPENT_____

1. Was the parking lot clean?   Y   N
2. Was the entryway free of debris?   Y   N
3. Were floors clean and aisles free of boxes?   Y   N
4. Were you acknowledged within 1 minute?   Y   N
5. If not, how long before you were acknowledged _____
6. Were all employees wearing nametags?   Y   N
7. Were items attractively displayed?   Y   N
8. Were prices easy to locate?   Y   N
9. Were shelves clean and dust free?   Y   N
10. How many employees did you see? _____
11. What were they doing? _____
12. Name and description of salesperson who assisted you

_____
13. Was the salesperson attentive?   Y   N
14. What question did you ask? _____
15. What was their response? _____
16. What did you purchase? _____
17. Name and description of cashier_____
18. Did the cashier smile and make eye contact?   Y   N
19. What was their greeting ?_____
20. Were you offered any additional items?   Y   N

Please explain any "No" answers.

Write a minimum of two paragraphs regarding your experience.

SAMPLE EVALUATION

GROCERY STORE

NAME_____DATE SHOPPED_____
STORE_____ADDRESS_____
TIME ENTERED_____TIME DEPARTED_____
AMOUNT SPENT_____

Was the parking lot clean?   Y   N
How many carts were loose in the lot?   _____

PRODUCE DEPARTMENT

Name or description of employee_____
What question did you ask? _____
What was their response? _____

BAKERY DEPARTMENT

Name or description of employee_____
What question did you ask? _____
What was their response? _____

CASHIER

How many cashier lines were open? _____
How many Express lines were open?_____
How many cashier lines does this store have?_____
How many people were in the longest line? _____
Name or description of employee_____
How were you greeted? _____
How long did you wait (in minutes and seconds) from the
time you got in line until you were greeted? _____
Were you charged correctly?   Y   N
Which restroom did you visit? _____
Was it clean and properly supplied? _____

ADDITIONAL COMMENTS:

DID YOU NOTICE?

BUILDING EXTERIOR
      Appearance
      First impression
      Sufficient parking
      Landscaping
      Lighting

INTERIOR
      Cleanliness
      Clean tables/displays
      Ambiance
      Restrooms

EMPLOYEES
      Names/descriptions
      Greetings
      Friendliness
      Timings
      Uniforms
      Nametags

FOOD OR PRODUCTS
      Appearance
      Descriptions

SATISFACTION
      Would you return?

"The worst thing you can do is meet expectations one time, fall short another, and exceed every now and then. I guarantee you'll drive your customers nuts and into the hands of the competition first chance they get."

    Blanchard, Ken and Bowles, Sheldon *Raving Fans A Revolutionary Approach to Customer Service* New York: William Morrow and Company, Inc.

IMPORTANT POINTS
TO REMEMBER

Don't ever compare shops. Treat each assignment as if it is your first visit to that establishment.

Answer every question on the questionnaire. Leave no blanks.

Explain every NO answer.

Proofread your work and use the spellchecker on your word processing program. If you are filling out a form online, you can download a free spellcheck program at www.iespell.com.

Never make recommendations unless specifically asked by the Mystery Shopping company.

Itemized receipts are almost always required.

Again, if you make a commitment to complete a shop--follow through.

SUGGESTED ITEMS TO BRING WITH YOU.

A watch, preferably with a second hand.

Two pens and a small pad of paper.

Some shops will require additional items such as a timer or stop watch, digital thermometer, scale, tape recorder, video recorder, etc. Many of the Mystery Shopping companies will provide these extra tools when needed.

It is also a good idea to have a separate wallet to use if you will be paying cash. This way there will be no mix-up and you will always be able to determine if you actually received the correct change.

MYSTERY SHOPPING DO'S AND DON'TS

DO read your instructions carefully before doing your shop.

DO blend in. You don't want to be "spotted" or remembered.

DO dress appropriately. Look like the regular customer.

DO keep an open mind.

DO show a positive and friendly attitude

DO complete your assignment and questionnaire within the timeframe set by the Mystery Shopping company.

DO proofread your work.

DO enjoy your assignment!

DO NOT set up the employee for failure.

DO NOT take your paperwork into the establishment.

DO NOT ask a lot of questions.

DO NOT tell any employee that you are a Mystery Shopper.

DO NOT draw attention to yourself.

DO NOT be overly critical.

DO NOT use slang or contractions when writing reports.

RETAIL SHOPPER SCENARIO

Practice Exercise

Here are a few scenarios followed by sample evaluations which you may complete for practice.

It's 7 p.m. You approach the parking lot and observe that it is well lit and you feel safe. There are two soda cans and several pieces of litter at the entrance to the store. You enter the store and your first impression is that it is clean and organized.

Three employees are on the sales floor. One is drinking a soda and the other two are assisting customers. No one greets you and you browse the store for two minutes. You pass by the employee who is drinking soda and she does not acknowledge you. (She has short brown hair and wears glasses.) One of the other employees approaches you and says, "Hi. Can I help you find something?" She is not wearing a nametag. She is female and has long blonde hair worn in a ponytail. You tell her that you are looking for a pair of khaki pants. She asks questions to determine your size and style, and then escorts you to the display. She walks away. You look through the items and observe that the pants have sizes and price tags.

You then stroll to the shoe department where several shoe boxes are blocking the aisles. The carpet is stained and needs vacuuming. You go to the sale display and find a T-shirt you want to try on. You enter the dressing room. The mirror is clean and the room is tidy.

You decide to purchase the T-shirt and walk up to the employee at the cashier stand. She is female and has blonde, curly hair. She greets you with a smile and asks if you found everything.. She mentions the special sale they are having on handbags. Your transaction is completed flawlessly and you are thanked as you leave the store at 7:22 p.m.

RETAIL SCENARIO EVALUATION FORM

Complete the following evaluation based on the previous retail scenario.

Arrived _____ Departed_____ No. of employees____No. of customers____

Sales Associate name or description_____

Cashier name or description_____

Was the parking lot clean and well lit?   Y   N

Was the entrance clean and inviting?   Y   N

What were the employees doing? _____

Were you greeted and offered assistance?   Y   N

What question did you ask?_____

How did the employee respond?_____

Were you escorted to the product?   Y   N

Did the employee sell the product?   Y   N

Was the dressing room clean?   Y   N

Was the store well maintained?   Y   N

What did you purchase?_____

Was the cashier friendly?   Y   N

Please write a minimum of two paragraphs and explain any no answers.

RESTAURANT SHOPPER SCENARIO

Practice Exercise

You and your partner arrive at the parking lot at 12:15 pm. The landscaping is neatly trimmed and the restaurant entrance is clean. As you approach the door, it is opened for you and a hostess welcomes you.

You walk up to the reception podium and are greeted with a smile. The receptionist, Sally (wearing a nametag), asks how many are in your party and tells you there is a fifteen minute wait. You are seated at 12:30 by Phyllis. She walks you to your booth, sets the menus in the center of the table, and leaves.

Five minutes later your server comes by. He says, "Hi. I'm Peter. Can I get you something to drink?" Peter is wearing black pants and a freshly pressed white shirt, similar to the other servers. You order a diet soda and lemonade and receive them in two minutes. When Peter returns, he says, "Are you ready to order?" You ask him if there are any specials and he tells you about two special features: the Pasta with Chicken and the Grilled Trout. You place your order for the entrees and salads at 12:40 p.m.

You check the restroom and note that it is clean and has all the necessary supplies. You observe a female employee who is dressed in a beige pant suit. She has blonde shoulder length hair and is not wearing a nametag. She is interacting with the employees and also greeting customers. She is the manager.

Your salads arrive at 12:45. Some of the lettuce has brown spots. The entrees are delivered at 12:52 by Louis, the food runner. He asks which of you ordered the pasta dish and sets the plates in front of you, warning that they are hot. The entrees are served in attractive, clean dishes and look colorful and delicious. The food runner removes your salad plates. Two minutes later, Peter comes by to check on your satisfaction. He offers to refill your drinks. You ask for additional napkins and he brings them to you one minute later.

You push your plates back after fifteen minutes and Peter comes by immediately. He asks if you saved room for dessert. When you decline the dessert, Peter then presents you with a check and thanks you for coming in.

As you leave the dining area, Sally says, "Have a nice afternoon." You exit at 1:20 p.m.

RESTAURANT SCENARIO EVALUATION FORM

Time in_____Time out_____% of guests in restaurant_____
Lunch___ Dinner___

Name or description of Host

Name or description of Server

Was the lobby clean and inviting?   Y   N

Were you seated immediately?   Y   N

If you waited for seating, was the quoted time accurate?   Y   N

How long before your server greeted you at the table?_____

Did the server make any suggestions?   Y   N

How long before you received your drinks?_____

How long before your appetizers were served?_____

How long before you received your entrees?_____

How long before your server checked back?_____

Was your server attentive?   Y   N

Did you observe a manager?   Y   N

Write a minimum of three paragraphs that tell a story from the time you arrived until you departed. Would you return to this location? Why or why not? Please be descriptive.

Be sure to fax or scan your itemized receipt.

COMMENTS ON
SCENARIO EXERCISES

Did you run across some problems while filling out the evaluations?

RETAIL SCENARIO EVALUATION

What criteria did you use to determine if the parking lot was clean? You are usually not given any specifics as to how many pieces of litter should be on the ground before you consider it clean. You must use common sense. If it was a windy day you might expect more litter. If there were three pieces of litter, would that be considered dirty? What if someone just dropped the litter a few minutes ago? I received an assignment once that asked me if the windows were clean. I asked the Mystery Shopping company for the definition of a dirty window. The answer, "If it turns you off, it's dirty."

How would you answer a question that was actually two different subjects? For instance, "Was the parking lot clean and well lit?" Unless both subjects were a YES, the answer would be NO. Then in your narrative you would explain the details such as, "The parking lot was clean but it was not well lit."

RESTAURANT SCENARIO EVALUATION

The evaluation asks if you were seated immediately. How does that question get answered? The hostess told you that there would be a fifteen minute wait and you waited fifteen minutes. Although you were seated in the appropriate amount of time, it would not qualify for "immediate seating." You did have to wait for fifteen minutes.

Did the server make suggestions? If the server asked, "Are you ready to order?" That would not qualify as a YES to that question. In order for that answer to be YES, specific items must be mentioned.

Success is about enjoying
what you do

6

BECOMING AN INDEPENDENT CONTRACTOR

Most companies will hire you as an independent contractor rather than as an employee.

TYPICAL
INDEPENDENT CONTRACTOR AGREEMENT

Most Mystery Shopping companies will hire you as an independent contractor. In other words, you are not an employee. You will become self employed. You will be given some forms to complete and sign. The first form will be an Independent Contractor Agreement. See the typical sample below.

The undersigned hereby enters into a certain arrangement with (Company) as of this date and agrees as follows:

1. The undersigned is an independent contractor and is not an employee, agent, partner or joint venturer of or with the company.

2. The undersigned shall not be entitled to participate in any vacation, medical or other fringe benefit or retirement program of the company and shall not make claim of entitlement to any such employee program or benefit.

3. The undersigned shall be solely responsible for the payment of withholding taxes, FICA and other such tax deductions on any earnings or payments made, and the company shall withhold no such payroll tax deductions from any payments due. The undersigned agrees to indemnify and reimburse the company from any claim or assessment by any taxing authority arising from this paragraph.

4. The undersigned and company acknowledge that the undersigned shall not be subject to the provisions of any personnel policy or rules and regulations applicable to employees as the undersigned shall fulfill its responsibility independent of and without supervisory control by the company.

Signed this   day of   20____

_____   _____
Independent Contractor   Company

CONFIDENTIALITY AGREEMENT

SAMPLE

In addition to the Independent Contractor Agreement, you may be asked to sign a Confidentiality Agreement. See a sample agreement below.

The undersigned agrees that he/she will not disclose any confidential information including but not limited to trade secrets, proprietary information, clients names, and any and all written and verbal information regarding assignments.

All designs, materials and statistical data belong to the company.

You will not make any copies unless specifically asked to do so.

You shall not disclose any information to any other individual.

Upon termination of this agreement, it is agreed that all requested materials be returned to the company.

Agreed to this _____day of _____, 20_____

_____   _____

Independent Contractor   Mystery Shopping Company

FORM W-9

TAXPAYER IDENTIFICATION NUMBER AND CERTIFICATION

One other form that will be required is an Internal Revenue Service Form W-9. This form is used to report income paid to you. You will be required to enter your name and address. You must also fill in your Taxpayer Identification Number (TIN). For individuals, this is your Social Security Number (SSN). For other entities, it is your Employer Identification Number (EIN).

The Mystery Shopping companies will provide you with a blank form (see sample next page) to fill out and sign. You will not be hired until you sign this form.

Form **W-9** (Rev. October 2007) Department of the Treasury Internal Revenue Service	**Request for Taxpayer** **Identification Number and Certification**	**Give form to the** **requester. Do not** **send to the IRS.**

Print or type
See Specific Instructions on page 2

Name (as shown on your income tax return)

Business name, if different from above

Check appropriate box: ☐ Individual/Sole proprietor ☐ Corporation ☐ Partnership
☐ Limited liability company. Enter the tax classification (D=disregarded entity, C=corporation, P=partnership) ▶ _____
☐ Other (see instructions) ▶

☐ Exempt
payee

Address (number, street, and apt. or suite no.)

Requester's name and address (optional)

City, state, and ZIP code

List account number(s) here (optional)

Part I   **Taxpayer Identification Number (TIN)**

Enter your TIN in the appropriate box. The TIN provided must match the name given on Line 1 to avoid backup withholding. For individuals, this is your social security number (SSN). However, for a resident alien, sole proprietor, or disregarded entity, see the Part I instructions on page 3. For other entities, it is your employer identification number (EIN). If you do not have a number, see *How to get a TIN* on page 3.

Note. If the account is in more than one name, see the chart on page 4 for guidelines on whose number to enter.

Social security number

or

Employer identification number

Part II   **Certification**

Under penalties of perjury, I certify that:

1. The number shown on this form is my correct taxpayer identification number (or I am waiting for a number to be issued to me), and

2. I am not subject to backup withholding because: (a) I am exempt from backup withholding, or (b) I have not been notified by the Internal Revenue Service (IRS) that I am subject to backup withholding as a result of a failure to report all interest or dividends, or (c) the IRS has notified me that I am no longer subject to backup withholding, and

3. I am a U.S. citizen or other U.S. person (defined below).

Certification instructions. You must cross out item 2 above if you have been notified by the IRS that you are currently subject to backup withholding because you have failed to report all interest and dividends on your tax return. For real estate transactions, item 2 does not apply. For mortgage interest paid, acquisition or abandonment of secured property, cancellation of debt, contributions to an individual retirement arrangement (IRA), and generally, payments other than interest and dividends, you are not required to sign the Certification, but you must provide your correct TIN. See the instructions on page 4.

Sign **Here**	Signature of U.S. person ▶	Date ▶

General Instructions

Section references are to the Internal Revenue Code unless otherwise noted.

Purpose of Form

A person who is required to file an information return with the IRS must obtain your correct taxpayer identification number (TIN) to report, for example, income paid to you, real estate transactions, mortgage interest you paid, acquisition or abandonment of secured property, cancellation of debt, or contributions you made to an IRA.

Use Form W-9 only if you are a U.S. person (including a resident alien), to provide your correct TIN to the person requesting it (the requester) and, when applicable, to:

1. Certify that the TIN you are giving is correct (or you are waiting for a number to be issued),

2. Certify that you are not subject to backup withholding, or

3. Claim exemption from backup withholding if you are a U.S. exempt payee. If applicable, you are also certifying that as a U.S. person, your allocable share of any partnership income from a U.S. trade or business is not subject to the withholding tax on foreign partners' share of effectively connected income.

Note. If a requester gives you a form other than Form W-9 to request your TIN, you must use the requester's form if it is substantially similar to this Form W-9.

Definition of a U.S. person. For federal tax purposes, you are considered a U.S. person if you are:

● An individual who is a U.S. citizen or U.S. resident alien,

● A partnership, corporation, company, or association created or organized in the United States or under the laws of the United States,

● An estate (other than a foreign estate), or

● A domestic trust (as defined in Regulations section 301.7701-7).

Special rules for partnerships. Partnerships that conduct a trade or business in the United States are generally required to pay a withholding tax on any foreign partners' share of income from such business. Further, in certain cases where a Form W-9 has not been received, a partnership is required to presume that a partner is a foreign person, and pay the withholding tax. Therefore, if you are a U.S. person that is a partner in a partnership conducting a trade or business in the United States, provide Form W-9 to the partnership to establish your U.S. status and avoid withholding on your share of partnership income.

The person who gives Form W-9 to the partnership for purposes of establishing its U.S. status and avoiding withholding on its allocable share of net income from the partnership conducting a trade or business in the United States is in the following cases:

● The U.S. owner of a disregarded entity and not the entity,

Cat. No. 10231X   Form **W-9** (Rev. 10-2007)

TAX INFORMATION

As previously noted, most Mystery Shopping companies will consider you an independent contractor. The following are excerpts from various sources and may or may not be applicable or accurate for your particular needs. Please consult your tax professional and attorney with any questions concerning how you should file your particular income tax and to determine what your status is according to state law.

The following guidelines are subject to change by the IRS.

Form 1099
Companies are required to provide you with a Form 1099 if you make $600 or more per year for their company. Keep in mind, however, that you are still required to declare this income even if you've made less than the $600 and do not receive the 1099 unless you are exempt from filing income taxes altogether. You are required to file a Schedule C for your total Independent Contractor income. Refer to the IRS guidelines to see who must file. Even if you do not have to file a return, it may be to your advantages if you are due a refund or are eligible for earned income credit.

The IRS lists Forms and Instructions that are available online at http://www.irs.gov The IRS also offers Fill-In Forms that allow you to enter information.

Filing your Return
You must file a return using the 1040 form if you had net earnings from self employment (i.e., you worked as an Independent Contractor). Because you will be receiving self-employment earnings you cannot use Forms 1040EZ or 1040A. You can use the handy Fill-in Form 1040. For more details, see the information under 1040s at the IRS website.

Profit or Loss from a Business
You may need to use Schedule C to report profit or loss from a business you operated or a profession you practiced as a sole proprietor. You need to include all income earned as an Independent Contractor, even if you did not receive a 1099. All income you receive from any company you work for will be reported to the IRS even if it is a nominal amount.

Schedule C is also used when you itemized and deduct your business expenses. These are the current operating costs of running your business. To be deductible, a business expense must be both ordinary and necessary. An ordinary expense is one that is common and accepted in your field of business, trade or profession. A necessary expense is one that is helpful and appropriate for your business, trade or profession. You may deduct your business expenses on Schedule C or the simpler Schedule C-EA if your annual business expenses are under $2,500, you do not have inventory or employees, you use the cash method of accounting, and if certain other requirements are met. For additional requirements and details review the Schedule C Instructions. For more details about business expenses refer to IRS Publication 535.

Car and Truck Expenses
If you use your car in your job or business and use it only for that purpose, you may deduct the entire cost of its operation (subject to certain limits).

If you use your vehicle for both business and personal purposes, you may deduct only the cost of its business use. Your expenses, divided between business and personal use, can be based on the miles driven for each purpose. You can generally figure the amount of your car's business expense one of two ways: the standard mileage rate, which fluctuates yearly, or the actual expense method. The documentation you need for these expenses can be found in IRS Publication 583.

Home Deductions
If you are self employed, use Form 8829 to figure your business use of the home deductions and report those deductions on Schedule C Form 1040. For details see IRS Publication 587 Business Use of Your Home

Self-Employment Tax
You must file Schedule SE and pay the SE tax if your total net earnings from self employment were over $400. From the bottom line of Schedule C, get the combined total net earnings. The SE tax is a Social Security and Medicare tax primarily for individuals who work for themselves. It is similar to the Social Security and Medicare taxes withheld from the pay of most wage earners. For more details see the Self Employment Tax Publication 533 and the SE Instructions.

Fees paid for tax advice related to your business and for preparation of the tax forms related to your business are deductible on Schedule C.

SHOPPING ASSIGNMENT TRACKING

FORM

Since you are now self employed, you will need some method to track your reimbursements and payments. You will not normally send out invoices because usually your completed evaluation forms will serve as an invoice for the Mystery Shopping company.

There are many ways to keep records and the following is one method that you might find useful. This form will also allow you a final accounting at the end of the year by showing your actual earnings and expenses.

An explanation on the form's use follows on the next page.

1.	2.	3.	4.	5.	6.	7.	8.
DATE SHOPPED	MS COMPANY	RETAILER CITY	ASSIGNMENT #	GROSS PAID	Minus EXPENSES	NET RECEIVED	DATE PAID
1/1	XYZ	Bill's Café Chicago	A303	65.00	50.00	15.00	3/5

You can also keep track of your gas mileage by adding another column. Or, keep a log in your car that indicates date, starting and ending mileage, and location visited. As an Independent Contractor you can choose to deduct mileage from your taxes at the current IRS rate.

SHOPPING ASSIGNMENT TRACKING

Explanation on how to use this form

In the first column, DATE, enter the date you performed the shop.

In the second column, MS COMPANY, enter the name of the Mystery Shopping company that gave you the assignment.

In the third column, enter the name of the particular store you visited and their location.

In the fourth column, enter the assignment number which was given to you with your assignment instructions.

In the fifth column, enter the gross amount you will receive for this assignment. For instance, if you went out for dinner and were to be reimbursed $50 and in addition, you were to receive $15 to fill out the forms, your gross would be $65.

In the sixth column, enter your expenses. For instance, if you spend $50 for your dinner, you would enter that amount in the expense column.

In the seventh column, enter the amount you were paid over and above your reimbursement. In this instance, it would be $15.

In the eighth column, enter the date you received payment from the Mystery Shopping company.

You can add one more column which would be to track your mileage. You are rarely reimbursed by the company for your mileage, but you may be able to deduct it from your income taxes at the end of the year as an expense.

I keep a gas mileage book in my car. When I leave for an assignment I enter the date, beginning mileage and location of assignment. When I return, I enter the ending mileage. At the end of the year I add up the mileage and base my calculations on that amount.

COMPANY CONTACT RECORD

It is important to keep a record of the companies that you have registered with. Many companies have similar sounding names and it is easy to become confused.

You may wish to keep a log of the companies as follows.

- DATE SIGNED UP

- MYSTERY SHOPPING COMPANY NAME

- LOCATION (You will need to know their time zone in case you want to call them)

- PHONE NUMBER

- WEBSITE ADDRESS

- SCHEDULER NAME

- SCHEDULER EMAIL

- YOUR SHOPPER ID NUMBER

- YOUR PASSWORD

You will be given a shopper ID number and password for each company with which you will be working. It is vitally important to keep these numbers handy as, without them, you may not be able to access the website and input your reports. And since I would suggest that you sign up with as many companies as you possibly can—I doubt that too many of us are able to recall the numerous different shopper identification numbers.

You may choose to keep a record on a computer database. on index cards, or in a special binder. Find a system that works best for you. I keep my list in a special section in my address book.

7

ADDITIONAL HELPFUL INFORMATION

Being a Mystery Shopper will pave the way for you to positively impact a broad range of businesses.

SOME ACTUAL QUOTES
FROM OUR EXPERIENCES

See if you can spot the best type of responses.

SOME DIRECTIONS THAT WERE PROVIDED ON THE PHONE

1. "If you're on 6th, we'll be on your right."

2. "I'm new to the area. I don't know."

3. "I think you take Interstate 5. We're near downtown."

4. "If you're coming south on Interstate 5, take the 6th Avenue exit and turn right. We're three blocks from the freeway on the east side."

GREETING FROM HOSTS AT FINE DINING RESTAURANTS

1. "Two?"

2. "Bill, can you seat these guys?"

3. "Welcome to Sea House. Do you have a reservation this evening?"

SERVER GREETINGS

1. "Do you know what you want?"

2. "Can I get you guys a drink? Water?"

3. "Good evening. Can I get you started with a drink from the bar? Our Martinis are world famous."

RESPONSES RECEIVED WHEN ASKING SERVERS FOR AN ENTRÉE RECOMMENDATION

1. "The chicken is rather bony; the pork is greasy. I'd try the lamb."

2. "I don't know. I'm a vegetarian."

3. "We are known for our prime rib, but the steaks are also very popular."

RESPONSES TO QUESTIONS AT RETAIL STORES

1. "What? I never heard of it."

2. "We don't sell that."

3. "We don't carry that but perhaps we can special order it for you."

AFTER ASKING FOR A GIFT RECOMMENDATION FOR A NEPHEW

1. "How would I know what he likes? I don't know him."

2. "I'll be with you as soon as I finish stocking this section."

3. "Let me escort you to our gift department. We have a huge selection. Does he have any particular hobbies?"

CASHIER GREETING COMMENTS

1. "Next."

2. "$10.50"

3. "Is this yours?"

4. "Good evening. Did you find everything alright?"

PHONE CALL TO FRONT DESK AT A RESORT HOTEL TO RESOLVE A PROBLEM. WE FOUND A LARGE COCKROACH IN OUR ROOM.

1. "Is it dead or alive? It'll be on its back of its dead. Can you toss it in the toilet?"

2. "I'm so sorry. We'll have someone come to your room immediately."

GROCERY STORE RESPONSES

1. "If we have any, they'd be in Aisle 5."

2. "Hey Joe, do we have any corn on the cob? This lady wants to know."

3. "A new shipment came in this afternoon. I'll bring you some."

PHONE RESPONSES WHEN CALLING A RESTAURANT

1. After one ring: "Yo."

2. After one Ring: "Sally's. Press 1 for catering, 2 for Sally, 3 for Fred. All other calls please hold. ONE MINUTE LATER: We value you as a customer. Continue holding."

3. After two rings: "Thank you for calling Sally's Steakhouse. This is Andrea speaking. How may I help you?"

If you guessed that the best response was the last answer for each category, you were right. Congratulations.

––––––––––

"Being on hold is insulting. How much of your life do you want to spend being on hold?"
> Glen, Peter *It's Not My Department! How to Get the Service You Want, Exactly the Way You Want It* New York: William Murray and Company, Inc.

DO NOT REVEAL
THAT YOU ARE MYSTERY SHOPPER

Your identity as a Mystery Shopper is to remain a secret. Unless otherwise instructed you are NEVER to reveal that you are on an assignment as a Mystery Shopper. The secret is to act "natural."

My husband and I recently dined at a high end restaurant and saw a large sign behind the hostess podium. It said, "WATCH FOR MYSTERY SHOPPERS." It brought a smile to my face because I wondered what they were watching for. Of course it was to remind the employees to be aware at all times and to be providing excellent service to everyone because they never know who the Mystery Shopper is.

After 25 years of assignments, I did finally get caught recently. This came about in a way I never would have imagined. Here's the story.

I had an assignment at a computer store. They were part of a large chain of smaller computer stores. I performed the assignment as instructed and was impressed with the knowledge of the employees. I wrote up the evaluation, received my payment, and went about my daily affairs. Several months later my computer crashed. I remembered the store and decided to bring the computer to them for repair. The employees were helpful, and after several tests it was determined that the computer was beyond repair. I then bought a new computer and the employee, out of the kindness of his heart, said that he would be glad to transfer my old files to the new computer at no charge. Not being able to resist such an offer, I accepted... Can you see what's coming?

I stood by watching the files go from one machine to the other. I had designated my files with content appropriate names – according to what they contained. When it came to the M's – up popped my files titled, *Mystery Shopping.* The employee looked at the title, then turned to look at me and said, "Are you the Mystery Shopper?" I sheepishly said, 'Oh, those are old files. I used to do that years ago for a fast food restaurant."

FREQUENTLY ASKED QUESTIONS

Let's review some important items.

Why do companies use Mystery Shoppers?
As a Mystery Shopper, you provide valuable information to the company regarding customer service and adherence to company policies.

Are you hired by the retail store or the Mystery Shopping company?
In most cases you will be hired by the Mystery Shopping company as an independent contractor.

What type of people are companies looking for?
The average customer who frequents that particular store.

What will make us better shoppers?
Read the instructions and follow the guidelines

If I purchase something do I need a receipt?
You will need the itemized receipt, not just your charge receipt.

Is it okay to work for more than one Mystery Shopping company?
By all means, sign up with many different companies. Choices are always good.

How are my reports used?
Often the employees receive bonuses and special recognition for a good report. The corporate offices of the retailer also get to see an overall chart of what is happening throughout all of their stores. They can track trends easily and adjust training programs to deal with shortcomings.

Can I take children with me on assignments?
Be careful and considerate when bringing along children. You want the employee to do their best job and a child might be a distraction for you and the employee.

Should the Mystery Shopping company be located in the city where I reside?

Mystery Shopping companies are located throughout the world. They do not have to be located in your city in order to offer assignments there.

If I turn down assignments, will this hurt my chances of more jobs?

No. You do not have to accept every assignment that is offered to you. However, if you accept an assignment and then do not perform, you may not be used again by that company. They are depending on you to keep your commitment.

How long should I keep notes and reports?

Keep them at least until you have received payment for the assignment. Some companies ask that you keep them for six months or a year. You also need some of the paperwork for tax purposes.

Will I be hired as an Employee or as an Independent Contractor?

In most cases you will be an Independent Contractor.

Will I be reimbursed for my gas?

No. You will rarely receive mileage expenses, except of course when you shop a gas station!

How long do I have to wait to get paid?

Every company has a different pay schedule. When you become a shopper you will learn about their policies. Reimbursement can take anywhere from one week to three months. You can make the decision before accepting an assignment.

WORDS OF ADVICE FROM THE EXPERTS

I asked a few owners of Mystery Shopping companies if they would offer some words of advice for the readers of this book. I hope you will find their comments informative. Because of space limitations, I have limited the comments to excerpts from three different companies. I think you will find they cover a broad spectrum of the industry.

From Clay S. Carlos, President of ACRA, Inc.

Having owned and operated a small secret shop company for over ten years, I have watched the industry change before my eyes. Some of these changes have been positive, but other changes concern me.

The single largest change in the industry has been the advent of the Internet. The Internet allows companies to find shoppers, assign jobs, and provide reports all with the push of a few buttons. Prior to the computer age, scheduling shops, mailing instructions, and submitting reports could take weeks, if not months.

However, with this change, I have noticed many disturbing trends. Many larger companies are starting to rely on automated scheduling services. This scheduling process drastically reduces the need for personnel, but it does not always choose the best shopper. Many shoppers are chosen - by a computer - for a job simply because they were first to respond to a posting or an email. Not only is this new age of scheduling unfair to shoppers, but it is not in the best interest of the client. Assigning a job to the first person to respond to a posting does not take into account a shopper's experience, qualifications, or writing ability. For this reason, the quality of the reports supplied by these companies is often very disappointing to their clients.

Although the Internet has changed the industry forever, I am far more concerned with the direction we are headed regarding payment for shops. Secret shopping is a wonderful way in which shoppers can earn a few dollars in their spare time. With the exception of a few devoted, lucky, and hardcore shoppers, this has never been an industry that provided enough compensation to earn a living. For the most part, the average shopper uses secret shopping as an opportunity to supplement their income.

... Due to the competition that has been created by many new companies throwing their hat into the arena, price has become a major motivation in wooing new clients or obtaining clients from other secret shop companies. Established shoppers, who have been in the industry for years, are balking at the low compensation. On the other hand, new shoppers, who are desperate to break into the industry, are accepting assignments with ridiculously low fees.

Regarding compensation for assignments, there are two very important aspects that should be considered. From the shopper's perspective, do not accept an assignment simply to get your foot in the door. As stated above, many companies are assigning shops on a first come, first serve basis, and they do not have any loyalty to their shoppers. Accepting shops with low fees is simply feeding the very companies that are cutting costs to clients simply to undercut the competition. From the perspective of the company looking to start a secret shop program, do not choose a secret shop service based solely on price. Instead, ask the following questions; What system do you employ to choose shoppers? What interaction do you have with your shoppers? How do you ensure a quality and professional shop report? Do you edit reports for accuracy or inconsistencies? What efforts do you take to make shoppers loyal to your company?

...I truly believe that secret shops are one of the best training tools a company can use to evaluate their employees and ensure adherence to corporate policies and procedures. Not only are these reports inexpensive (as compared to other corporate expenditures), but they are conducted by an unbiased, third party, who is often a regular, every day customer. In summary, I would like to remind shoppers of the responsibility they are undertaking when accepting an assignment. Your feedback is not only critical to the individual you are shopping, but it is important to the future of the company who is requesting the shop, and it is a reflection of the secret shop company that gave you the assignment.

Although secret shopping sounds fun and exciting, it is not an easy task. It requires a self starter who gets the job done no matter what obstacles they are faced with in their everyday life. It also requires an eye for detail, complete focus on the task at hand, dedication, and motivation. Secret shopping is not for those interested in visiting the mall for a fun day of shopping. Instead, it is a "job" that requires the full attention and focus of an individual, and the ability to "tune out" surrounding distractions while concentrating on the task at hand.

From Jill Burns, President of Creative Strategies

Even if mystery shopping is new to you, know that the industry has been around a very long time. My grandmother worked at Macy's Herald Square store in New York City for many years. It was known as the world's largest department store. My grandmother remembered being "shopped" even way back then!

Today, there are many mystery shopping firms in the U.S. and throughout the world. Some are very large, some are small. Most have specialties - be it retail, banking, utilities, restaurants, movie theaters, hotels, insurance companies, cruise lines, airlines, casinos, law firms, convenience stores, amusement parks. Even some state and local governments use mystery shopping to assess their staff's performance. While the specific reasons and goals behind using a mystery shopping firm may vary, ultimately, there are always three winners. The business benefits from the feedback about how their staff does their job, the staff benefits from recognition and rewards they receive for doing a great job (or perhaps some additional training if it's warranted), and hopefully, many customers benefit from the organization's concerted effort to satisfy their needs and exceed their expectations.

Having spent 25 years working in corporate customer service in a variety of industries including mystery shopping, and seeing first hand the power great customer service has to increase any business' bottom line, it is disappointing when staff members don't display the service-oriented characteristics that are an inherent part of their job and the reason why the company hired them in the first place.

Case in point. While conducting an evaluation at a restaurant, a server contest was going on that would have yielded a $100 bonus for suggesting one of the restaurant's many draft beers to the shopper. The restaurant wanted its servers to let diners know about it - they were even running a special on it. Even with the incentive and the fact that it was such an easy thing to mention, our server said nothing to us about it.

Many years ago, one of our clients thought they'd caught one of our shoppers when they found a little note pad at a table that had been inadvertently left behind. They were sure they remembered who the people were and smirked with delight that they'd been so savvy about finding it and showing it to us. When they gave us the pad, we could see that many comments were written about meals from a variety of restaurants. Initially we were disappointed to think that one of our shoppers had done something we ask them not to do (that is, take notes at the table - a definite no, no). But upon closer inspection, we determined that it must have been a newspaper food critic who was conducting an evaluation! We were the ones who had smiles on our faces when we left knowing that we had not been, as our clients thought, out-foxed!

Finally, here's a BIG "no no." A shopper who was conducting her first evaluation with us was unhappy with their dining experience. While we want all our shoppers to have a fun time and experience great service and delicious food, sometimes things don't always turn out as planned. Needless to say, instead of "saving it for the report," our shopper made an issue of the problems they had and made a special point of contacting the general manager of the restaurant the following day to complain. The manager sent her certificates for a complimentary meal. Not only was the evaluation no longer anonymous and forgettable, but we retrieved the certificates from her and gave them back to our client. As a shopper, discretion is paramount. Unless requested to do so by the firm you work with, do not complain as it makes you anything but forgettable.

Special concerns:

1. Your honesty and integrity is paramount to the mystery shopping firm(s) you work with.

2. Information must be accurate, detailed and complete.

3. Find assignments that match your abilities and skills. If you are not a great writer, then look for shops that don't require too much of it.

4. Read all e-mails that are sent to you (in their entirety) and when in doubt, ask questions.

5. If you can't perform an assignment as scheduled, make informing your scheduler a priority. While everyone understands that sometimes things come up, it is irresponsible to accept an assignment and fail to perform it and even worse when you don't communicate it.

6. Avoid offering suggestions in your reports, telling the business what they should or should not do. Your purpose as a shopper is to report on what you observed and experienced.

7. Unless you are requested to do so, avoid complaining about anything (problems with the food unless something is inedible, problems with service, being overcharged, being undercharged, etc.) - save it for the report!

From James Duthie, Online Marketing & Communications Manager Gapbuster Worldwide

GAPbuster Worldwide is the world's largest mystery shopping company. Here's why:

- We were established in 1994 and have been working in mystery shopping for over 24 years.
- We operate in over 30 countries throughout the world.
- We have a global team of more than 120,000 mystery shoppers.
- We have offices located in Chicago, London, Tokyo, Melbourne, Frankfurt & Copenhagen.
- We work with some of the largest brands in the world.

Tips for mystery shoppers:

We've put together a short list of the attributes that we look for in mystery shoppers.

Reliability - Just like any other job, if you pull out of a work commitment at the last minute you may have to deal with the consequences. Companies monitor assignment cancellations very closely and mystery shoppers that prove to be unreliable are removed from shopping lists. On the up side shoppers that prove their reliability over a period of time are often rewarded with more assignments and priority access to the most popular assignments.

Accuracy - Each mystery shopping assignment has its own specific requirements. Mystery shopping certification programs help you to become familiar with these requirements. However, you'll also need to download and review a set of instructions and a questionnaire. This paperwork will outline of the specific requirements of the assignment. You'll need to complete your assignment in accordance to these guidelines to ensure that it is accepted and valid.

Discreetness - As a mystery shopper it is your job to go unnoticed. Most companies will void the results of a mystery shopping assignment if you are identified. You're likely to receive the red carpet treatment if they realize that they are being evaluated.

A good memory - Some mystery shopping assignments require you to make up to 70-80 observations. And this can include remembering up to 3 people's names and descriptions.... all in the space of about 10 minutes.

<u>Internet savvy</u> - the best mystery shopping companies have complete online systems through which you can conduct all your mystery shopping needs. For this reason you'll need to be fairly savvy with your use of the Internet and online operating systems.

<u>Responsiveness</u> - Good mystery shoppers check their email at least a couple of times a day. A mystery shopping company may get in contact with you for a range of different reasons, and in most cases they're after a fairly swift response. Shoppers that are responsive to their needs are often placed on the preferred mystery shoppers list.

<u>Objectivity</u> - as a mystery shopper you aren't getting paid to get on your high horse to critique customer service experiences. Rather you are simply being asked to observe and report the service that you receive. The best mystery shoppers are able to witness the events before them rather than judge them.

HARD TO BELIEVE BUT TRUE STORIES

My husband does occasional Mystery Shopping and tends to be very selective of his assignments. There was an assignment one day for a restaurant that had a drive through window for take-out service as well as dining room service. He was going to be in the area of the restaurant on that particular day and I convinced him to accept the shop. I said, "It's a drive-thru. What could be easier?" I emphasized the importance of getting the itemized receipt and he told me not to worry, that he would handle it. The day of the shop, I phoned him three times to tell him not to forget the receipt, stressing that we would not be reimbursed without it. I was looking forward to 6:00 when he would come home with our dinners and I had the table set. He walked in and waved a piece of paper in front of me saying, "See, I've got the receipt." "Great," I said. "Let's sit down and eat." "Oops," he said. "I forgot the food."

My partner and I had lunch at an upscale restaurant and our server, although attentive and pleasant, acted nervous. We had the impression that this may have been his first day. The portions at this restaurant were very large and we couldn't finish everything on our plate. The server asked if he could box up our leftovers and we readily agreed. When we got home and I went to put the leftovers in the refrigerator, I saw that he packed the leftovers, dishes and all, in the container.

My instructions for a retail shop said that I must get the employee's name. The employee I dealt with had an "attitude" and was not at all friendly. She did not smile, she did not even make eye contact. She was not wearing a nametag and her name was not on the receipt. After we finished the transaction I asked, "By the way, what is your name?" Her response was, "Why do you want to know?" I thought to myself, "Because you need training," but instead I said the first thing that came to mind. "My neighbor's cousin works here and I thought you might be her." The employee then asked, "What's her name?" I was being put into a corner, but played it through and said, "Heather." The employee's response was, "Heather is due in at 1:00." You're right. I never did get her name but I did have an accurate description.

USEFUL ONLINE RESOURCES

Some of the Mystery Shopping websites will require you to have certain software. The following offer free trial or free downloads which you will find helpful.

FLASH PLAYER
Enables you to view certain websites
http://www.macromedia.com/shockwave/download/download.cgi?P1_Prod_Version=ShockwaveFlash

SPELL CHECK PROGRAM FOR INTERNET EXPLORER
Helps you with your proofreading by performing spell checks
www.hotlingo.com

SPELL CHECK PROGRAM TO CHECK SPELLING ON WEBSITES
www.iespell.com/download.php

ADOBE ACROBAT READER
Enables you read view PDF files
www.adobe.com/products/readstep.html

INTERNET EXPLORER
For current users of Internet Explorer: Upgrade the latest version
www.microsoft.com/windows/ie/default.mspx

COUNT LINES, WORDS, CHARACTERS
www.harmonyhollow.net

VIEWERS FOR WORD AND EXCEL
www.microsoft.com

THESAURUS
www.thesaurus.com

WINZIP (compress files)
www.winzip.com

And here are addresses of other useful sites.

INTERNAL REVENUE SERVICE
www.irs.gov

PAYPAL (online bank)
www.paypal.com

TOO GOOD TO BE TRUE

SOME INSIGHT INTO SCAMS
AND MALICIOUS SPYWARE

All of us are inundated with email offers, newspaper ads, and other gimmicks to "get our money." The more we use our computers, the more we open ourselves up to falling victim to the scam artists who thrive on our trusting nature.

Although Mystery Shopping is a legitimate occupation, there are many schemes aimed at Mystery Shoppers and I would like to ask you to take a few moments to read the following pages. Become a savvy shopper and computer user. Don't fall for the scams.

Here are some excerpts from: **Federal Trade Commission Bureau of Consumer Protection Office of Consumer & Business Education**

The Secrets of Mystery Shopping Revealed. *Do you love to shop? If so, you may be tempted by unsolicited emails or newspaper ads that claim you can earn a living as a secret or mystery shopper by dining at elegant restaurants, shopping at pricey stores, or checking into luxurious hotels. But, according to the Federal Trade Commission (FTC), the nation's consumer protection agency, marketers who promise lucrative jobs as mystery shoppers often do not deliver bona fide opportunities.*

The truth is that it is unnecessary to pay money to anyone to get into the mystery shopper business. The shopping certification offered in advertising or unsolicited email is almost always worthless. A list of companies that hire mystery shoppers is available for free; and legitimate mystery shopper jobs are on the Internet for free. Consumers who try to get a refund from promoters of mystery shopping jobs usually are out of luck. Either the business doesn't return the phone calls, or if it does, it's to try another pitch

In the meantime, the FTC says consumers should be skeptical of mystery shopping promoters who:
- *Advertise for mystery shoppers in a newspaper's 'help wanted' section or by email. While it may appear as if these companies are hiring mystery shoppers, it's much more likely that they're pitching unnecessary — and possibly bogus — mystery shopping "services."*
- *Sell "certification." Companies that use mystery shoppers generally do not require certification.*

114

- *Guarantee a job as a mystery shopper.*
- *Charge a fee for access to mystery shopping opportunities.*
- *Sell directories of companies that provide mystery shoppers.*

If you think you have encountered a mystery shopping scam, file a complaint with your local consumer protection agency, the Better Business Bureau, your State Attorney General, or the FTC (ftc.gov).

FTC Charges Defendants Misrepresented Available Jobs, Potential Income. *An operation that told consumers they could be hired as mystery shoppers and earn a substantial income, and the telemarketing firm working for them, are facing Federal Trade Commission charges that their claims about job availability and income potential were deceptive. The FTC also charged the mystery shopping operation with contempt for violating a previous FTC order, and is seeking redress for consumers, who lost millions of dollars.*

The FTC alleged that in exchange for the $99.95 fee for one year of service, consumers thought they would be trained and certified as mystery shoppers, and would gain access to job postings available through the company, with enough paid assignments available to ensure a steady part-time or full-time income. Instead, consumers received a worthless certification and access to mystery shopping assignments that had been posted by other companies, who were unrelated to the defendants.

FTC Alleges Deceptive Selling of Bartending and Mystery Shopping Program. New Charges Brought Against Repeat Offenders. *Two individuals and two corporations, who allegedly took in over $5 million from consumers, are charged by the Federal Trade Commission with using deceptive marketing tactics when selling their at-home certification programs for bartenders and mystery shoppers. The FTC alleges the defendants promised jobs as bartenders and mystery shoppers, but delivered only useless certification programs and general information on potential employers. According to the FTC, the defendants' business activities not only violated federal law, but also the terms of an October 2001 court order entered against the two individual defendants in an earlier Commission case. One defendant has agreed to a lifetime ban to settle the FTC's charges.*

Phishing: *Are you one of many who have received an e-mail, text message, or telephone call, supposedly from your credit card/debit card company directing you to contact a telephone number to re-activate your card due to a security issue? Vishing operates like phishing by persuading consumers to divulge their Personally Identifiable Information (PII), claiming their account was suspended, deactivated, or terminated. Recipients are directed to contact their bank via a telephone number provided in the e-mail or by an automated recording. Upon calling the telephone number, the recipient is greeted with "Welcome to the bank of ......" and then requested to enter their card number in order to resolve a pending security issue*

Please beware—spam e-mails may actually contain malicious code (malware) which can harm your computer. Do not open any unsolicited e-mail and do not click on any links provided. If you have a question concerning your account or credit/debit card, you should contact your bank using a telephone number obtained independently, such as from your statement, a telephone book, or other independent means.

Don't fall for this 'mystery shopper' check scam*. You receive a letter saying you've been selected to become a "mystery shopper" at an amazing $125 an hour. Enclosed is a $3,150 cashier's check and instructions to deposit it in your bank and then visit a local department store customer-service desk and pose as someone buying a Money Gram (with funds from your own personal check or credit card) to wire $2,825 to a relative in Canada. The cashier's check amount covers the cost of the Money Gram, including the department store's fee, and $250 for you for two hours of work, which includes filling out a survey on the service you received. It sounds like the quickest $250 you'll ever make.*

But after you complete the assignment, you'll soon realize you've been had. Within weeks the financial institution where you deposited the cashier's check will notify you that it is fraudulent and that you must pay back the $3,150. What makes this scam particularly disturbing is how legitimate it appears. The documents are business-like, and the cashier's check carries the name and address of an actual financial institution. The toll-free number, however, belongs to the scam artists. If would-be shoppers call it to verify the deal, they'll receive assurance of the check's "authenticity."

You might get such a letter after you post a resume on email job sites or respond to an online work-at-home promotion. The Federal Trade Commission has issued a warning about this and other check scams.

And last, I would like to caution you about responding to unfamiliar web ads. Here is an excerpt from an article in THE WALL STREET JOURNAL.

Web ads are becoming a delivery system of choice for hackers seeking to distribute viruses over the Internet...Just going to a site that shows such an ad can infect a user's computer.

An example they illustrated: A virus in a banner ad on a legitimate website automatically switched visitors to a website that downloaded "malware" – malicious software designed to attack your computer.

....estimates the banner ad was on the legitimate site for at least 24 hours and infected 50,000 to 100,000 computers before the company removed it.

My personal rule of thumb is that I never respond to ads of any kind. I may go to a legitimate mystery shopping company's website and see some banner ads and side ads advertising all types of things. My business is with the legitimate mystery shopping company – not with the ads. And I will NEVER respond to the ads. Let's say for instance that Legitimate Mystery Shopping Company ABC has a website you use to find out about assignments in your area. You would want to visit the website to learn more about the assignments to see if you are interested in them. Good. Now, while you're on their website pages, you see some ads pop up advertising other things such as RELIABLE WORK AT HOME, INTERNET TYPING, STUFFING ENVELOPES, EARN $100 AN HOUR AS A MYSTERY SHOPPER. Oh Oh. They may sound tempting, but do you know who these other companies are? Just because they've placed their ads on a legitimate website does not mean that they are legitimate. Be careful. Why take a chance? To play it safe, my advice is to ignore those surrounding ads or at the very least, check them out before clicking on them.

The U.S.Federal Trade Commission (FTC), the nation's consumer protection agency, has hundreds of free consumer publications on issues related to credit, online safety, fraud, identity theft, and health and fitness, among many other topics. Most publications are available in Spanish and English. All are free.

Here's How to Place an Order: *For limited quantities of publications - 1-49 copies per title - call 1-877-FTC-HELP. You can also view, save, print and copy publications at <u>www.ftc.gov/consumer</u> or send your name, organization, address, telephone number, the titles you want - along with the quantities of each - to: Consumer Response Center, Federal Trade Commission*
600 Pennsylvania, NW, H-130, Washington, DC 20580

8

DIRECTORIES

Mystery Shopping websites organized especially for you.

DIRECTORY INFORMATION

You will find the following resources an invaluable tool as you begin your journey. A listing here is not an endorsement by me. Please feel free to contact me at Info@MysteryShoppersTraining.com with any corrections, additions, or recommendations for future inclusion.

These resources are divided into different sections as described below.

MYSTERY SHOPPING COMPANIES
These are the companies to which you will apply.

MYSTERY SHOPPING ASSOCIATIONS
Associations whose membership includes Mystery Shopping Companies.

MYSTERY SHOPPERS' WEBSITES
Websites you might find useful for job listings and general information about Mystery shopping.

SCHEDULERS' WEBSITES
Schedulers are the people that handle your assignments and will be your link to several mystery shopping companies.

MERCHANDING, MARKET RESEARCH.
There are so many other fun ways to earn part time income.

FOCUS GROUPS
And, if you have not already discovered Focus Groups, I would suggest you visit www.marketsdirectory.com/focmkti.htm for a list of focus groups in your area. For those of you unfamiliar with focus groups, here is a definition: A small group selected from a wider population and sampled, as by open discussion, for its members' opinions about a particular subject or area.

MYSTERY SHOPPING COMPANIES

You can apply directly to any of these Mystery Shopping companies. Most companies prefer that you contact them via their website rather than calling on the phone. Go directly to their websites and you will be able to read about the company, learn their policies, and determine whether or not you want to sign up with them. You will then fill out your application on line.

After you have completed the application they will either inform you that they will contact you when shops are available, or they may immediately have you sign an Independent Contractor Agreement, a Non-Disclosure Agreement, and a W-9 Form. At that time they may also provide you with a Shopper Identification Number and a password to use for accessing your account.

Some companies send you emails when they have shops in your area, some of the companies list the shops directly on their websites and you can select the ones you are interested in. This will all be explained to you when you sign up with them.

I am frequently asked to include a listing of the types of shops that each Mystery Shopping company performs. Please be aware that their particular account information is confidential and I cannot list their clients.

What is "Sassie" Shop?

As you view the DIRECTORY OF MYSTERY SHOPPING COMPANIES, you will see that many different companies have "Sassie" in their address. Sassie is a program that many Mystery Shopping companies use. SassieShop.com and SurfMerchants are the publishers of the Sassie Mystery Shopping system software. They do not schedule shops or process payments to Mystery Shoppers (they only provide support for system-wide technical issues).

A & M BUSINESS SERVICES
www.ambussvcs.com

A CLOSER LOOK
www.a-closer-look.com

A CUSTOMERS POINT OF VIEW
www.acpview.com

A STEP ABOVE
www.serviceevaluations.com

A TOP SHOP
www.atopshop.com

ABSOLUTE ADVANTEDGE
www.absoluteadvantedge.com

ACE MYSTERY SHOPPING also known as
ASSOCIATE CONSUMER EVALUATIONS
www.acemysteryshopping.com

ADVANCED FEEDBACK
www.advancedfeedback.com

ADVANCED PHONE UPS
http://phoneups.com

AIM FIELD SERVICE
www.patsaim.com

ALCOPS also known as
ALLIED CORPORATE PROTECTIVE SERVICE
www.alcops.com

ALERT SHOPPERS
www.williams-jamal.com

ALEXANDRIA'S MARKETING
www.alexandriasmarketing.com

ALL STAR CUSTOMER SERVICE
www.mysteryshoppingexperts.com

ALOHA SOLUTIONS
www.alohasolutions.net

AMUSEMENT ADVANTAGE
www.amusementadvantage.com

ANN MICHAELS & ASSOCIATES
www.ishopforyou.com
www.annmichaelsltd.com
www.sassieshop.com/2annmichaels

ANONYMOUS INSIGHTS
www.a-insights.com

ANONYMOUS SHOPPER & ASSESSMENTS OF PITTSBURGH
www.asapittsburgh.com

ARC RESEARCH
www.arcresearch.com

ARCHON DEVELOPMENT
http://demo.archondev.com
This site will reach approximately15 affiliate
Mystery Shopping companies

ARDENT SERVICES
www.ardentservices.com

AT RANDOM COMMUNICATIONS.
www.arllc.com

AT YOUR SERVICE MARKETING
www.aysm.com

ATH POWER CONSULTING CORPORATION
Also known as COURTESY COUNTS
www.athpower.com
www.athpoweronline.com
www.sassieshop.com/2ap123

AUDITOR SERVICE
www.auditorservice.com (Spanish)

AUTOMOTIVE INSIGHTS
www.automotiveinsights.com

AVALA MARKETING GROUP
www.avalamarketing.com

B BUSINESS SOLUTIONS
http://bizshoptalk.com

BARE ASSOCIATES
www.baievaluators.com
www.baiservices.com
www.sassieshop.com/2bareusa
www.sassieshop.com/2bare

BARRY LEEDS & ASSOCIATES
www.barryleedsassoc.com

BASS COMPANY
www.bassreports.com

BESTMARK
www.bestmark.com

BEYOND HELLO
www.hellomirror.com
www.sassieshop.com/2beyondhello

BEYOND MARKETING GROUP (BMG)
www.beyondmarketinggroup.com

BIG K
www.bigk.com.mx (Mexico)

BMA BEST MARKET AUDITS also known as
BETTER MARKETING ASSOCIATES
www.mystery-shopping.com

BOROUGHS RESEARCH AGENCY
www.boroughsresearch.net

BUSINESS RESEARCH GROUP INC
www.brgus.com

BUSINESS EVALUATION SERVICES
www.mysteryshopperservices.com

BUSINESS INSIGHTS
www.businessinsights.com

BUSINESS RESEARCH LAB
www.busreslab.com

BYERS CHOICE
www.ByersChoiceInc.net

CALIFORNIA MARKETING SPECIALISTS
www.sassieshop.com/2californiamarketing

CAMPUS CONSULTING
www.shopaudits.com

CAPSTONE RESEARCH
www.capstoneresearch.com

C-CHEX
www.c-chex.com

CERTIFIED MARKETING/REPORTS
www.certifiedreports.com

CHECK MARK
www.checkmarkinc.com

CHECKER PATROL
www.checkerpatrol.com

CHECKUP MARKETING
www.checkupmarketing.com

CIRCLE OF SERVICE.
www.circle-of-service.com

CIRRUS MARKETING CONSULTANTS
www.cirrusmktg.com

CKA CONSUMER GROUP
CONSUMER KNOWLEDGE ANALYSIS
www.ckagroup.com

CLIENT FIRST ASSOCIATES
www.cf-associates.com

COMPLIANCE SOLUTIONS WORLDWIDE
www.sassieshop.com/2msint

CONFERO
www.conferoinc.com
www.sassieshop.com/2confero

CONSUMER CONNECTION / CONSUMER CRITIQUE
www.consumerconnection.net
www.consumercritique.com

CONSUMER IMPRESSIONS
www.consumerimpressions.com

CONSUMER KNOWLEDGE ANALYSIS
www.ckagroup.com

CONSUMER PULSE
www.consumerpulse.com

CONSUMER RESEARCH GROUP (CRG)
www.crg2000.com

CONSUMER RESEARCH GROUP (CRG)
www.crg-web.com

CONSUMER RESEARCH GROUP (CRG)
www.thecrg.com
www.crgms.com

CORPORATE RESEARCH INTERNATIONAL
(Formerly EMPLOYER EVALUATORS)
www.mysteryshops.com

CORPORATE RISK SOLUTIONS
www.sassieshop.com/2crs

COUNT ON US
www.ucountonus.com

COURTESY COUNTS
See also ATH POWER CONSULTING CORPORATION
www.courtesycounts.com

COYLE HOSPITALITY GROUP
www.coylehospitality.com

CREATIVE IMAGE ASSOCIATION, INC
www.creativeimage.net

CREATIVE MARKETING CONCEPTS
www.getcreativemarketing.com

CREATIVE STRATEGIES
www.strategz.com

CRITIQUE INTERNATIONAL also known
www.critiqueinternational.com

CROSS FINANCIAL GROUP
www.crossfinancial.com

CUSTOMER FIRST
FIRST POINT RESOURCES
www.customer-1st.com

CUSTOMER SERVICE EXPERTS
www.customerserviceexperts.com
www.sassieshop.com/2shopcse

CUSTOMER SERVICE PERCEPTIONS
www.csperceptions.com

CUSTOMER SERVICE PROFILES
www.csprofiles.com

CUSTOMERIZE
www.customerize.com
www.sassieshop.com/2customerize

CV MARKETING RESEARCH also known as
SENSUS RESEARCH
www.cv-market.com
www.sensusshop.com

CYBER SHOPPERS
ROPER NOP MYSTERY SHOPPING
www.cybershoppersonline.com

DATA QUEST LTD.
www.dataquestonline.com

DATATRON
www.usd-datatron.com

DAVID SPARKS AND ASSOCIATES
www.sparksresearch.com

DEVON HILL ASSOCIATES
www.devonhillassociates.com

DIVERSIFIED CORPORATION SOLUTIONS
www.divcorp.com
www.sassieshop.com/2dcs

DOUGLAS STAFFORD INTERNATIONAL
www.douglasstafford.com

DRAUDE MARKETING
www.draudemarketing.com

DSG ASSOCIATES
www.dsgai.com

DYNAMIC ADVANTAGE
www.dynamic-advantage.com

DYNAMIC SERVICE GROUP
www.dynamicservicegroup.com

ELLIS, PARTNERS IN MYSTERY SHOPPING
www.epmsonline.com

ELRICK AND LAVIDGE
See TNSI

EMYSTERY SHOPPER
www.edigitalresearch.com

EPINION AMERICA
www.epinionamerica.com

ESP EVALUATION SYSTEMS
www.espshop.com

EXAMINE YOUR PRACTICE
www.examineyourpractice.com

EXCEL SHOPPING & CONSULTING
www.excelshoppingandconsulting.com

EXPERT SHOPPING PROFESSIONALS
www.expertshoppingpros.com

EXTRA EYES NATIONWIDE, INC.
www.extraeyes.net

EYES R US
www.eyesrusinc.com
www.sassieshop.com/2eyesrus

FEEDBACK PLUS INC
www.feedbackplusinc.com

FIELD FACTS
www.fieldfacts.com

FIRST POINT RESOURCES
See CUSTOMER FIRST

FOCUS ON SERVICE
www.focusonservice.com

FRANCHISE COMPLIANCE
www.sassieshop.com/2franchisecompliance

FREEMAN GROUP SOLUTIONS
http://shopper.freemangroupsolutions.com

GAME FILM CONSULTANTS
www.mysteryshopinc.com

GAP BUSTER
www.gapbuster.com

GLOBALCOMPLIANCE
www.gcsresearch.com

GOODWIN & ASSOCIATES
www.mysteryshopperprogram.com

GRANTHAM, ORILIO AND ASSOCIATES
Also known as
SYSTEM CHECK BY ORILIO & ASSOCIATES
www.sassieshop.com/2goa

GRAYMARK SECURITY
www.graymarksecurity.com

GREEN AND ASSOCIATES INTERNATIONAL
Associated with ShopNChek
www.greenandassociates.com

GREET AMERICA
www.greetamerica.com
May charge a fee.

GREET AMERICA
www.ga-mysteryshopper.com

GUEST CHECK
www.theguestcheck.com
may charge a fee

HARRIS TEETER
www.sassieshop.com/2harristeeter

HIDDEN CONCEPTS
www.hiddenconcepts.com

HILLI DUNLAP ENTERPRISES
www.dunlapenterprises.com

HMI ASSOCIATES
www.hmiassociates.com

HOLLANDER, COHEN & MCBRIDE
www.hcmresearch.com

HOSPITALITY SERVICES
www.hsoneinc.com

HOTEL SHOPPING NETWORK
www.hotelmysteryshopper.com

HOWARD SERVICES also known as
SERVICE SLEUTHS
www.servicesleuths.com

HR & ASSOCIATES
www.hrandassociates.com

IC DECISION SERVICES
Division of National In-Store Service Company
www.iccds.com

ICU ASSOCIATES
www.icuassociates.com
www.lpinnovations.com

I-SPY MYSTERY SHOPPER
www.i-spy-ms.com

IMAGE CHECKERS
www.imagecheckers.com

IMAGINUS
www.imaginusinc.com

IMEDGEXPERTS
www.imedgexperts.com

IMYST
www.imyst.com

IN TOUCH SURVEY SYSTEMS
www.intouchsurvey.com

INFOTEL also known as
QUANTUM SYSTEMS
www.infotelinc.com

INLAND RETAIL SERVICES
www.inlandretailservices.com

INSTANT REPLY INC
www.mysteryshopservices.com

INSULA RESEARCH
www.insularesearch.com

INTELLISHOP also known as INSITE
www.sassieshop.com/2intellishop

JANCYN EVALUATION SHOPS
www.jancynonline.com
www.sassieshop.com/2jancyn

JC & ASSOCIATES
www.jcandassociates.com

JKS SERVICES
www.jksinc.com

JM RIDGWAY
www.jmridgway.com

KANE-BENSON & COMPANY
www.theshoppingcompany.com

KEN RICH RETAIL GROUP
www.ken-rich.com

KINESIS-CEM
www.kinesis-cem.com

KIRANDT GROUP
www.kirandt.com

LE BLANC & ASSOCIATES
www.mleblanc.com

LINNABARY AND ASSOCIATES
www.linnabary.com

LOSS PREVENTION ASSOCIATES
www.lpassociates.com

M VENTIX INC.
www.mventix.com

MACPHERSONMYSTERYSHOPPING
www.macphersonmysteryshopping.org.uk

MANAGEMENT CONSULTANT GROUP
www.managementconsultantgroup.com

MARITZ MARKETING RESEARCH
www.virtuoso.maritzresearch.com

MARKET RESEARCH
www.marketresearchdallas.com

MARKET TRENDS
www.markettrends.com

MARKET VIEWPOINT
www.marketviewpoint.com

MARKETING ENDEAVORS
www.marketingendeavors.biz
www.sassieshop.com/2me

MARKETING SYSTEMS UNLIMITED
www.members.aol.com/mktsys/
www.msultd.com

MARKETWISE CONSULTING GROUP
www.marketwi.com

MARKET FORCE INFORMATION
www.marketforce.com
(See also ShopnChek, SG Marketing, and
Speedmark)

MARS RESEARCH
www.marsresearch.com

MEASURE CONSUMER PERSPECTIVES
www.sassieshop.com/2msr

MELINDA BRODY & COMPANY
www.melindabrody.com

MERCANTILE SYSTEMS
www.sassieshop.com/2mercsurveys
www.mercsurveys.com

MICHELSON & ASSOCIATES
www.michelson.com

MINTEL
www.mintel.com

MYSTERY DINERS INC
www.mysterydinersinc.com

MYSTERY GUEST INC.
www.mysteryguestinc.com

MYSTERY SHOP INC
www.mysteryshopinc.com

MYSTERY SHOPPER USA
www.bmiltd.com

MYSTERY SHOPPERS
www.weneed.com

MYSTERY SHOPPERS
www.mystery-shoppers.com

MYSTERY SHOPPERS
www.sassieshop.com/2mysteryshoppers

MYSTIQUE SHOPPERS
www.sassieshop.com/2mystique

NATIONAL AUDITS
24 Wampum Road
Park Ridge, NJ 07656
Phone: 210 782 0714

NATIONAL INVESTIGATION BUREAU
www.nationalinvestigation.com

NATIONAL SHOPPING SERVICE
www.nationalshoppingservice.com
www.nssmysteryshoppers.com

NATIONAL SHOPPING SERVICE NETWORK
www.mysteryshopper.net

NATIONWIDE SERVICES GROUP
www.nationwidesg.com
www.sassieshop.com/2nis

NEW IMAGE MARKETING LTD
www.nimltd.com

North America MSS/HDE
www.dunlapenterprises.com
www.sassieshop.com/2hillidunlap

NORTHWEST LOSS PREVENTION CENTER
www.nwlpc.com

NSITE, INC
www.nsiteinc.com

OPINIONS, LTD.
www.opinionsltd.com

OSD CREATIVE BUSINESS SOLUTIONS
www.osdsolutions.com

PACIFIC RESEARCH GROUP
www.pacificresearchgroup.com

PEAK TECHNIQUES
www.peaktechniques.com

PERCEPTION STRATEGIES
www.perstrat.com

PERCEPTIVE MARKET RESEARCH
www.pmrresearch.com

PERFORMANCE EDGE
www.pedge.com

PERFORMANCE IN PEOPLE
www.performanceinpeople.com

PERSON TO PERSON QUALITY
www.persontopersonquality.com

PERSONNEL PROPHILES
www.ppiadvantage.com

PHANTOM SHOPPERS
www.phantom-shoppers.com

PHONE-SMART
www.phone-smart.net

PINKERTON FIELD RESEARCH see also
GLOBAL COMPLIANCE SERVICES
www.gcsresearch.com
www.ci.pinkerton.com

PREMIER SERVICE
www.premierservice.ca

PRIMO SOLUTIONS LLC
www.primosolutionsllc.com

PROFESSIONAL REVIEW SHOPPERS
www.proreview.com
www.sassieshop.com/2proreview

PROMOTION NETWORK
www.promotionnetworkinc.com

PROVE OF ORLANDO also known as
SHOPPERS CRITIQUE
www.proveoforlando.com

PULSE BACK
www.pulseback.com

QSI/QUALITY SERVICES
www.qsispecialists.com (Nevada)

QUALITY APPROACH
www.qualityapproach.com

QUALITY ASSESSMENTS
www.qams.com

QUALITY ASSURANCE CONSULTANTS
www.qacinc.com

QUALITY CHECK
www.undercovershoppers.com

QUALITY CONSULTANTS (QCI)
www.qualconsultant.com

QUALITY MARKETING
www.quality-marketing.com

QUALITY MARKETING GROUP
www.qmgrp.com

QUALITY SHOPPER
www.qualityshopper.org

QUALITY WORKS ASSOCIATES
www.qualityworks.com

QUANTUM SYSTEMS also known as INFOTEL
www.infotelinc.com

QUEST FOR BEST MYSTERY SHOPPERS
www.questforbest.com

QUICK TEST / HEAKEN
www.quicktest.com

QUINN MARKETING & COMMUNICATIONS
www.quinnmc.com

RAPID CHECK also known as
TNS MEDIA INTELLIGENCE
www.rapidchek.com

REALITY CHECK MYSTERY SHOPPERS
www.rcmysteryshopper.com

REFLECTIONS
www.reflectionsms.com

REGAL HOSPITALITY GROUP
http://shopper.regalhg.com

REMINGTON EVALUATIONS
www.remysteryshops.com

RESORT LOYALTY INC
www.resortloyalty.com

RESTAURANT COPS
www.restaurantcops.com

RESTAURANT EVALUATORS
www.restaurantevaluators.com
www.sassieshop.com/2resteval

RETAIL EYES
www.retaileyes.com

RETAIL TRACK
www.retailtrack.com

REYES RESEARCH
www.reyesresearch.com

RICKIE KRUH RESEARCH
www.rkrmg.com

RITTER AND ASSOCIATES
www.ritterandassociates.com

ROCKY MOUNTAIN RESEARCH
www.rockymm.com

ROPER NOP MYSTERY SHOPPING
www.cybershoppersonline.com
www.ropernopmysteryshopping.com

SALES BUILDERS MARKETING
www.sbmarketing.com

SALES QUALITY GROUP
http://shoppers.salesqualitygroup.com

SATISFACTION SERVICES
www.satisfactionservicesinc.com

SCHOLL MARKET RESEARCH
www.schollresearch.com

SCHRYVER ENTERPRISES
www.schryverenterprises.com

SECOND TO NONE
www.second-to-none.com

SECRET SHOP NET also known as
SERVICE INTELLIGENCE and
EXPERIENCE EXCHANGE
Acquired by Global Compliance
www.secretshopnet.com
www.experienceexchange.com

SECRET SHOPPER
www.secretshopper.com

SECRET SHOPPING SERVICES
www.secretshoppingservices.com
www.sassie.com/2sss

SENSORS QUALITY MANAGEMENT (SQM)
www.sqm.ca

SENSUS
www.sensusshop.com
www.cv-mystery.com

SENTRY MARKETING GROUP
www.sentrymarketinggroup.com

SERVICE ADVANTAGE INTERNATIONAL
www.servad.com

SERVICE CHECK
www.servicecheck.com
www.servicecheckreport.com

SERVICE ALLIANCE INC.
www.servicealliANCEinc.com

SERVICE CONNECTIONS
www.serviceconnectionsinc.com

SERVICEEVALUATION CONCEPTS
www.serviceevaluation.com

SERVICE EXCELLENCE
www.sassieshop.com/2serviceexcellence

SERVICE EXCELLENCE GROUP
www.serviceexcellencegroup.com

SERVICE EXCELLENCE GROUP
www.mysteryshopsplus.com
www.sassieshop.com/2servicex

SERVICE IMPRESSIONS
www.serviceimpressions.com
www.sassieshop.com/2serviceimpressions

SERVICE PERFORMANCE GROUP
www.spgweb.com
www.sassieshop.com/2serviceperformance

SERVICE PROBE
www.pwgroup.com/sprobe

SERVICE RESEARCH / SRC
www.serviceresearch.com

SERVICE SAVVY
www.servicesavvy.com
www.sassieshop.com/2servicesavvy

SERVICE SENSE
www.servicesense.com

SERVICE SLEUTHS also known as
HOWARD SERVICES
www.mymysteryshop.com
www.servicesleuths.com

SERVICE SOLUTIONS
www.ssishops.com

SERVICE TRAC INC
www.servicetrac.com

SERVICE X
www.sassieshop.com/2servicex

SG MARKETING
www.sgmarketing.com
www.sassieshop.com/2sgmarketing

SHADOW AGENCY
www.shadowagency.com

SHOP AUDITS also known as
CAMPUS CONSULTING
www.shopaudits.com

SHOPMETRICS
www.shopmetrics.com

SHOPNCHEK
www.shopnchek.com

SHOPPERS CONFIDENTIAL
www.shoppersconfidential.com

SHOPPERS CRITIQUE INTL
www.shopperscritique.com

SHOPPERS INC.
www.shopperjobs.com
www.shprsinc.com

SHOPPERS VIEW
www.shoppersview.com

SHOPPING BY MYSTERY
www.shoppingbymystery.com

SIGHTS ON SERVICE also known as
SECRET SHOPPER
www.mysteryshop.com

SIGNATURE INC
www.legendary.net

SIGNATURE WORLDWIDE
www.signatureworldwide.com

SINCLAIR SERVICE ASSESSMENTS
www.ssanet.com

SIPE & ASSOCIATES
www.sipeandassociates.com

SIX STAR SOLUTIONS
www.rockymn.com

SKIL CHECK
www.skilcheck.com

SNEAK PEAK MYSTERY SHOPPERS
www.spbon.com

SOUTHWEST MYSTERY SHOPPERS
www.secretshoppers.com

SPEEDMARK also known as GREEN and
SPEEDMARK VISION
www.speedmarkwcb.com
www.sassieshop.com/2green
Acquired by ShopNChek

SPIES IN DISGUISE
www.spiesindisguise.com

SPOT CHECK
www.spotcheckservices.com

STARTEX MARKETING SERVICES
www.startexms.com

STATOPEX
www.statopex.com

SUBURBAN ASSOCIATES
www.subassoc.com

SUPPORT FINANCIAL RESOURCES
www.serviceexperiences.com

SUTTER MARKETING
www.suttermarketing.com

TELL US ABOUT US, INC.
www.sassieshop.com/2tuau

TENOX APPRAISAL SYSTEMS
www.weshop4u.com

THEATRICAL ENTERTAINMENT SYSTEMS
www.tnsmi-tes.com/signmeup/signupmc.asp

TEST SHOPPER
www.testshopper.com

TEXAS SHOPPERS
www.texasshoppersnetwork.com

THE BENCHMARK COLLABORATORS
www.benchmarkco.com

THE BUYER'S VIEW
www.buyersview.net

THE GUEST CHECK
www.theguestcheck.com

THE SECRET SHOPPER COMPANY
www.secretshoppercompany.com

THE SERVICE QUALITY DEPARTMENT
www.service-quality.com

THE SHADOW AGENCY
www.theshadowagency.com

THE SHADOW SHOPPER
www.TSSOG.com

THE SOLOMON GROUP
www.thesolomongroup.com
May charge for training

TNS INTERSEARCH
www.sassieshop.com/2tns
www.mysteryclicks.com

TRANSUNION also known as
ZELLMAN GROUP
www.zellmangroup.com
www.sassieshop.com/2zellmangroup

TREND SOURCE
www.trendsource.com

ULTRA SHOPPER
www.ultrashopper.net

US MYSTERY SHOPPERS
www.usmysteryshoppers.com

VIDEO EYES
Affiliated with Bare Associates
www.videoeyes.net

VIEWPOINT
www.viewpointcr.com

WE NEED
www.weneed.com

WEB MYSTERY SHOPPERS
www.webmysteryshoppers.com

WEST SIDE DETECTIVES
www.westsidedetectives.com

WESTCOAST MYSTERY SHOPPING SERVICE
CANADA
www.westcoastmysteryshopping.com

Wise Shops
www.wiseshops.com
part of A Closer Look

MYSTERY SHOPPING ASSOCIATIONS

There are several associations that are for Mystery Shopping companies. These associations are instrumental in fostering growth of this industry. The associations offer the Mystery Shopping companies the opportunity to meet and discuss issues common to the industry. Mystery Shopping Providers Association is among the largest of these organizations.

Although, as a Mystery Shopper, you will not be joining these associations, you will want to become familiar with them as they offer a lot of useful information for shoppers. They not only offer certification, they also have lists of available Mystery Shopper assignments. You will look under your state and then city to see what shops are available. If there is anything that interests you, you can hit the reply button and let the scheduler know that you are interested in that assignment. You will also find direct links to the Mystery Shopping companies where you can fill out an application online to become a Mystery Shopper.

MYSTERY SHOPPING PROVIDERS ASSOCIATION
www.mysteryshop.org/shoppers

INTERNATIONAL ASSOCIATION OF SERVICE EVALUATORS
www.iasemysteryshop.com

INTERNATIONAL MYSTERY SHOPPING ALLIANCE
www.theimsa.com
International Mystery Shopping association

NATIONAL CENTER FOR PROFESSIONAL MYSTERY SHOPPERS INC
www.justshop.org

MYSTERY SHOPPER WEBSITES

There are many sites available for use by Mystery Shoppers. You will want to access them and choose your favorites. They offer helpful hints, tips, direct links to companies, and postings of mystery shops. The information is free. Some of the sites may offer items for sale, but do not feel you need to purchase anything. Take advantage of the useful and free information that is provided.

HOMETOWN
www.hometown.aol.com/mysteryshops/mystery.html
Message boards, mailing list, links for mystery
Shoppers

LILAS LOUNGE
www.lilaslounge.com
Forums and assignment links

MOM-MOM
www.mom-mom.com
Look under Making Money
Helpful links for Mystery Shoppers

MOM!MOM
http://topica.com/lists/mom
Mystery Shopping job leads

MS FREEDOM
www.msfreedom.org

MS OPENINGS
http://topica.com/lists/msopenings
Mystery Shopping lists

MYSTERY SHOP RESOURCES
www.mysteryshopresources.com
Resources, groups, tools, links

MYSTERY-SHOPPER
http://groups.yahoo.com/group/mystery-shopper
For Mystery Shoppers and schedulers to share

MYSTERY SHOPPING ASSIGNMENTS
www.mysteryshoppingassignments.com

MYSTERY SHOPPING SOLUTIONS
www.mystshopsol.com
Database for Mystery Shoppers

MYSTERY SHOPPERS TRAINING GROUP
www.MysteryShoppersTraining.com
Resources for training
Classes, books, videos, DVD's

POCKET CHANGE
www.pocket-change.com/mystery.htm
Direct links to mystery shop companies

QUALITY SHOPPERS
http://groups.yahoo.com/group/qualityshoppers
Mystery Shopping leads

QUIRKS
www.quirks.com
Mystery Shopping resources

SONYAS MYSTERY SHOPPERS
www.sonyasmysteryshoppers.com
Links to Mystery Shopping companies,
Helpful hints for shoppers

VOLITION
www.volition.com/forum or www.volition.com
Directories and useful links for Mystery Shopping
Direct links to Mystery Shopping companies
Daily lists of available assignments
Volition also offers many other types of opportunities and information at
no cost.

YOU CAN ALSO JOIN ANY OF THE FOLLOWING GROUPS AND LOOK
FOR THE MYSTERY SHOPPING LINKS.

www.onelist.com same as www.yahoo.com or www.smartgroups.com

Once you've joined the group, you will see a window that says SEARCH. I've listed four Mystery Shopping groups. There are many more. Input any of the following Mystery Shopping groups into that search window:
Mystery-shopper
Qualityshoppers
Shops-r-us
Shoppermatch

You will be directed to the group website and it will give you information about joining and accessing daily lists of shops that are available. There should never be a charge for this type of information.

SCHEDULING SERVICES WEBSITES

Some of the schedulers work for several companies, form alliances with other schedulers, and have set up their own websites. These sites list shops that are available from many different Mystery Shopping companies. Access them often and take advantage of the useful information they provide.

A CUT ABOVE
www.a-cutabove.com

BLD SCHEDULING SERVICES
www.bldschedulers.com

COAST TO COAST SCHEDULING
www.ctcss.com

DAWN HUNT
www.huntshomework.com
You will also have fun with Dawn's
list of current freebies at
Once you are on her site click on
DAWN'S DAILY DANDIES

DIRECT SCHEDULING SERVICES
www.directschedulingservices.com

JOB SLINGER
www.jobslinger.com

KERN SCHEDULING SERVICES
Also known as KSS INTERNATIONAL
www.kernscheduling.com

MYSTERY SHOPPER SOLUTIONS
www.mystshopsol.com

PALM SCHEDULING SERVICES
www.palmschedulingservices.com

QUALITY SCHEDULING
www.qualityscheduling.com

SHADOW SHOPPERS
www.shadowshoppers.com
They CHARGE a fee.

SHOPPING WITH DEBBY
www.shoppingwithdebby.com

TOTAL SCHEDULING RESOURCE
www.schedulingresource.com

VOLCANO SCHEDULING SERVICES
www.volcanoscheduling.com

BONUS MATERIALS
MARKET RESEARCH,
MERCHANDISING,
ONLINE OPINIONS

I have found that many of you who enjoy Mystery Shopping also enjoy new and creative ways to earn extra money. I've listed a few websites to get you started on some of these alternate methods.

AMERICAN CONSUMER OPINION
www.acop.com
www.americanconsumeropinion.com
online opinions

ATHENA RESEARCH GROUP
www.athenamarketresearch.com
online opinions

AW SURVEYS
www.awsurveys.com
surveys

BAKER STREET SOLUTIONS
www.bakerstsolutions.com
online opinions, products to test

BRAND INSTITUTE
www.biopensurveys.com

COMPEREMEDIA
351 W. Hubbard St 8th floor
Chicago, IL 60610-9833
Research Panel

CROSSMARK
www.crossmark.com
Merchandising

DELVE (formerly QSC)
www.delve.com
Online opinions

DIRECTIONS IN RESEARCH.
www.diresearch.com
Focus groups, marketing

DYNAMIC SERVICE GROUP
www.dynamicservicegroup.com
Merchandising

ELLIOTT BENSON
www.elliottbenson.com
Market research, opinions

EREWARDS
www.erewards.com

FIND FOCUS GROUPS
www.findfocusgroups.com
Learn about current focus groups in your area

FOCUS FORWARD
www.focusfwdonline.com
online opinions

HAUSER GROUP
www.hausernet.com
Decoy agents for mail tracking

J D POWER
www.jdpowerpanel.com
online opinions

MCMILLION RESEARCH SERVICES
www.mcmillionresearch.com
Surveys, test products

MINDFIELD ON LINE
www.mindfieldonline.com
Internet surveys

MOSAIC also known as IN STORE SOLUTIONS
www.infores.com
www.mosaic-infoforce.com
Auditing, data collection

NATIONAL ASSOCIATION OF RETAIL MERCHANDISERS (NARMS)
www.narms.com
Merchandising Association. Search for merchandising jobs in your state. Their website is user friendly and easy to navigate.

NICHOLS RESEARCH
www.nicholsresearch.com
Mock juries, research

NPD GROUP
www.npd.com
Opinion panels

PAT HENRY MARKET RESEARCH
www.thepathenrygroup
Product introductions, merchandising

PEOPLE PLUS
www.peopleplusinc.net
merchandising

PERSONAL OPINION
www.personalopinion.com
Focus groups

PINECONE RESEARCH
www.pineconeresearch.com
online surveys

PLAZA RESEARCH
www.iopinion.com
online opinions

PREMIUM RETAIL SERVICES
www.premiumretail.com
merchandising

PRISM RETAIL SERVICES
www.prismretailservices.com
Merchandising

PROMOTION NETWORK INC
www.promotionnetworkinc.com
Field marketing

R & R MARKETING
www.rrmarketingservicesinc.com

REPS MERCHANDISING
www.repsltd.com
Merchandising

RESEARCH INC
www.researchincorporated.com
Focus groups

RGIS
www.rgisinv.com
Inventory specialists

RQA INC
www.rqa-inc.com
Recalls, audits

SALES BUILDERS
www.sbmarketing.com
Merchandising

SAS STAFFING
www.sasstaffing.com
Merchandising, demos

SERV CORP INC.
www.servcorp.com
Demos

SOUTHERN EXPOSURE
www.southernexposure.us
sampling, couponing, merchandising

SPAR GROUP
www.sparinc.com

SSI MERCHANDISING
www.SSIMerchandising.com
Merchandising

STRATEGIC INSIGHTS
www.strategicinsightsinc.net
Surveys, market research

SUPERIOR PRODUCT PICKUP
www.productpickup.com
Product Retrievals

SURVEY SAVVY Division of LUTH RESEARCH
www.surveysavvy.com
Online surveys

THE ELEVEN AGENCY
www.t11a.com
Merchandising

9

WRAP-UP

CHECKLIST

- ✓ PREPARE YOUR SAMPLE PARAGRAPHS FOR THE APPLICATIONS

- ✓ OPEN A FREE PERSONAL PAYPAL ACCOUNT

- ✓ SEARCH FOR JOBS THAT ARE OF INTEREST TO YOU

- ✓ SIGN UP WITH AT LEAST 10 COMPANIES AS A STARTING POINT AND KEEP ADDING MORE AS TIME ALLOWS.

    1. BY VISITING THE VARIOUS JOB BOARDS, SCHEDULERS' SITES OR FORUMS SHOWN IN THE DIRECTORY SECTION

    2. OR BY APPLYING DIRECTLY AT THE MYSTERY SHOPPING COMPANY WEBSITES

- ✓ ONLY ACCEPT ASSIGNMENTS THAT YOU FEEL CONFIDENT YOU CAN COMPLETE

- ✓ DO A "PRACTICE RUN" A FEW DAYS BEFORE YOUR FIRST FEW ACTUAL ASSIGNMENTS TO GAIN CONFIDENCE

- ✓ READ AND FOLLOW THE INSTRUCTIONS

- ✓ SUBMIT YOUR REPORT AND RECEIPTS IN A TIMELY MANNER.

- ✓ ACCEPT MORE JOBS

- ✓ HAVE FUN